Schweitzer, George Keene, 1924–
The doctorate; a handbook, by George K. Schweitzer. Springfield, Ill., C. C. Thomas [1965]

vii, 106 p. illus. 24 cm.

Bibliography: p. 98–99.

1. Degrees, Academic. I. Title.

THE DOCTORATE

A Handbook

THE DOCTORATE

A Handbook

By

George K. Schweitzer, Ph.D., Sc.D.

Professor of Chemistry
The University of Tennessee
Knoxville, Tennessee

CHARLES C THOMAS · PUBLISHER
Springfield · Illinois · U.S.A.

Published and Distributed Throughout the World by
CHARLES C THOMAS • PUBLISHER
BANNERSTONE HOUSE
301-327 East Lawrence Avenue, Springfield, Illinois, U.S.A.
NATCHEZ PLANTATION HOUSE
735 North Atlantic Boulevard, Fort Lauderdale, Florida, U.S.A.

Library of Congress Catalog Card Number: 65-15811

With THOMAS BOOKS careful attention is given to all details of manufacturing and design. It is the Publisher's desire to present books that are satisfactory as to their physical qualities and artistic possibilities and appropriate for their particular use. THOMAS BOOKS will be true to those laws of quality that assure a good name and good will.

Printed in the United States of America
N-1

Introduction

SINCE about the turn of the century the number of doctoral degrees awarded has increased with each passing year. This increase is a reflection of a growing demand for highly-educated persons in practically all professions. Something over 25,000 doctorates were granted this past academic year.

This handbook was written to set forth in brief compass the history, the present status, the etiquette, and the ceremony of the various doctoral degrees. It is intended for all holders of doctorates and for those who come into contact with them. Its functions are to inform, to explain, and to clarify.

Gratitude is due many: Mrs. Betty Britton who typed and read proof, my wife Verna who cared and criticized, Dr. Kevin Sheard who shared his knowledge of academic regalia, the five cap and gown companies mentioned in Appendix 6 for counsel, the numerous respondents to surveys (foreign cultural attaches, officers of professional societies, doctoral holders, college and university registrars), Roy Craik Kollenborn who did editing, and Eric George, Miss Deborah Keene, Miss Ruth Anne, and D. R. Binker for assistance.

G.K.S.

Contents

THE DOCTORATE

A Handbook

CHAPTER ONE

The History of the Doctorate

I must acquire the absurd title of "Doctor." It will not make me a hair the better, but as times go no man can be counted learned unless he is styled "Doctor." If the world is to believe in me, I must put on the lion's skin. I have to fight with monsters and I must wear the dress of Hercules.

— — — *Adapted from* ERASMUS *(1466-1536).*

The Term Doctor

IN RECENT years, more than 25,000 earned doctorates of various types have been awarded annually in the United States. These degrees have been in a wide variety of disciplines including the natural sciences, the social sciences, the arts, the humanities, medicine, theology, education, dentistry, veterinary medicine, and many others. From the general trend, the number of persons attaining to doctoral degrees in future years will continue to increase.

The term doctor is derived from the Latin *docere,* which means "to teach." Its essential and earliest meaning is simply "one who teaches." The same Latin root is found in other English words such as doctrine, docile (teachable), and document. Later the word came to be used for persons who did not practice the art of teaching.

The term doctor was applied by the early Romans to those who gave public lectures on philosophical subjects. It was one of the titles used in the early church for teachers in the catechetical schools, who were called *doctores audientium.* Some of the most learned teachers were termed doctors of the church, *doctores ecclesiae.*

The Early Schools

The beginning of the twelfth century marked the emergence of the West from darknesses of many kinds. A vibrant upsurge of new ideas, outlooks, and techniques occurred about this time. Learning came to be highly-prized. A widespread desire for instruction resulted. To meet the demand, many teachers set themselves up to provide tutelage. Any teacher who gathered a number of students around him was called a doctor or a master.

In Northern Europe and England, cathedral schools flourished and multiplied. Each of them was under the supervision of a chancellor or head teacher appointed by the bishop. To teach at or near the cathedral schools, one needed the approval of the chancellor. Such approval, the *licentia docendi,* the license to teach, was granted on evidence that the applicant had knowledge of the subjects which he proposed to teach. This evidence usually was in the form of a recommendation from the doctor (teacher) under whom the applicant had studied.

In Italy, a somewhat different pattern evolved. Teachers had gathered into certain towns, there being few cathedral schools in this part of the West.

Some of the larger centers of teachers, either around cathedrals or in town centers, were those at Rheims, Chartres, Laon, Tours, Orleans, Paris, Bologna, Salerno, and Oxford. These centers received students from all over the western world. Their instruction was in the basic liberal arts: language, oratory, logic, mathematics, astronomy, music, bible, philosophy, and perhaps some theology, medicine, and law. Some of the centers gradually came to specialize in certain disciplines in addition to the basic general training. Paris excelled in theology, Bologna in law, Salerno in medicine.

The teachers in these centers, known as doctors or masters, organized themselves into trade unions after the pattern of medieval guilds. These academic, scholastic, or pedagogical guilds adopted regulations governing the admission of new doctors or masters into their ranks. The rules included stipulations concerning training and examinations. The teaching license was awarded only after the requirements had been met. It was through such supervision that the original teaching license became the prototype of the university degree. It was, in a fashion, the first doctor's degree, since it established a man as a "doctor" on the basis of a set pattern of training and accomplishments. In Northern Europe and England these licenses were granted by the cathedral school chancellors. In Italy and elsewhere in Southern Europe, the doctor's guilds granted their own licenses.

The First Universities

By the years from about 1130 to 1160 two centers of instruction had attained sufficient size, prestige, and organization to be termed universities in approximately the modern sense of the word. These schools, in Paris and in Bologna, were acknowledged by reputation and general consent to be *studia generalia,* that is, schools of far more than local significance. Because of this recognized excellence, a doctor of Paris or Bologna was authorized to instruct in any center. He was granted the *jus ubicunque docenti,* the right to teach anywhere.

The university at Bologna became the model for many others which arose in the southern regions of Europe in the thirteenth and fourteenth centuries. The university in

Paris served as the pattern for Oxford, the third school of generally recognized excellence in the twelfth century. Paris also was the model for many other universities founded later in Northern France, England, and Central Europe. The map on the facing page shows the locations of the most important universities of the thirteenth and fourteenth centuries, with the approximate dates of their founding in parentheses. Most of the universities founded after the three earliest (Paris, Bologna, Oxford) were certified as universities by a papal or imperial bull. Such an edict also granted the privilege of conferring the *jus ubicunque docenti.*

Although the guilds had made "doctors" of students, the first university doctorates were probably the Doctor of Civil Law and the Doctor of Canon Law awarded by Bologna in the twelfth century for the completion of its courses of study in law. The South European schools adopted the practice. As other faculties came into existence, at Bologna and elsewhere, the title of doctor appears to have been used in all fields.

In Paris, the prevailing title in the faculties of theology, medicine, and arts was originally master, while the title doctor predominated in law. These distinctions, however, were not rigid. The titles master and doctor were used interchangeably for graduates in the various fields. The situation was similar at Oxford and other schools patterned after Paris, but the title of doctor gradually replaced that of master in the higher faculties of theology, law, and medicine, master being retained in the lower faculty of arts.

The doctor's degree moved into a position of superiority to the master's degree, the master of arts in many schools becoming prerequisite to a doctorate in the other fields. In a number of universities, an advanced curriculum in the

B: Bologna (1160)
Bu: Buda (1389)
C: Cambridge (1209)
Cl: Cologne (1385)
Co: Coimbra (1290)
Cr: Cracow (1364)
E: Erfurt (1378)
F: Florence (1321)
G: Grenoble (1339)
H: Heidelberg (1386)
M: Montpellier (1220)
N: Naples (1224)
O: Oxford (1167)
P: Paris (1160)
Pa: Padua (1222)
Pe: Pecs (1367)
Pr: Prague (1348)
R: Rome (1303)
S: Salamanca (1243)
T: Toulouse (1229)
V: Vienna (1365)

IMPORTANT UNIVERSITIES OF THE THIRTEENTH AND FOURTEENTH CENTURIES

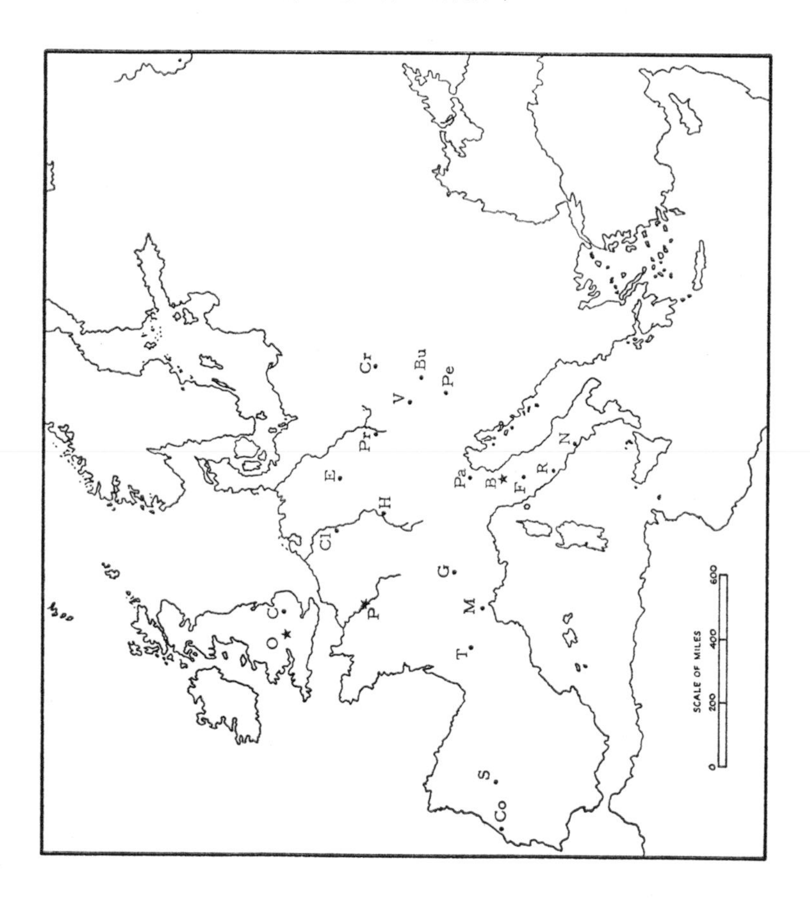

faculty of arts was inaugurated, its name being changed to the faculty of philosophy. A doctor of philosophy degree began to be awarded, sometimes being combined with the master of arts, especially in the German universities.

By the beginning of the fourteenth century, the doctorate or mastership had become a highly-significant acknowledgement of intellectual nobility. It occupied a distinct place in medieval society. The doctor's degree was taken by many who did not remain in academic work and often possessed the character of a license to exercise (outside the university) the expertise represented by the degree. This was especially true in such areas as law, medicine, and theology.

The title of doctor thus began to take on a broader connotation than that of teacher. It came to signify a learned man in a given field of endeavor. By the advent of the sixteenth century, many disciplines became the subjects of doctoral degrees, doctorates being awarded or recognized in civil law, canon law, both laws, theology, medicine, arts, philosophy, mathematics, logic, rhetoric, grammar, surgery, music, and even astrology.

The Curricula

Due to the diverse historical orgins of the different universities, the precise degree programs varied considerably. Yet, because of the general unity of medieval society, the subject matter of the various fields was usually quite similar. In some cases it was possible for a student to do his study at one university and to take his degree at another. The total time required for the doctorate ranged from six to twenty years, depending on the field of study, the starting date, and the university. In many schools, particularly those patterned after Paris, it was necessary to earn a master's degree or at least to do considerable study in the arts before proceeding to the doctorate in the so-called higher faculties of theology, law, and medicine. In other universities, the student apparently entered directly into the specialized curriculum, the necessary general educational background being included in the course of study.

The former pattern, as seen in many places in the fifteenth century, involved four to six years of study in the faculty of arts (also known in some places as the faculty of philosophy) leading to the master of arts degree. About midway in his course of study, the student became a bachelor of arts and advanced to the status of a teaching assistant.

Following his license to teach in the arts and his master of arts degree (conferred simultaneously or close together), six to sixteen years of further study were required for the doctorate in theology, law, medicine, or other higher disciplines. Again, midway in this course the student passed through the bachelor's degree and received the teaching license in the discipline near the termination of the course.

The doctoral degree in theology was apparently the most difficult one. At least it was the most time consuming, sixteen years of study beyond the master of arts being required at certain schools at certain times. In general, doctorates in the other fields could be earned in less time, usually six to eight years. These periods seem quite lengthy, until one considers the divergence of theory and practice, the exceptionally low educational level of beginning students, and the operation of bribery and laxity in medieval universities.

The early programs of study for the various degrees are impressive. For the master of arts, the course might include studies in logic (from Aristotle, Boethius, Porphyry, Gilbert de la Porree); in grammar and rhetoric (from Priscian, Donatus, Gilbert, Cicero, Ovid); in ethics, metaphysics, psychology (all from Aristotle); in astronomy (from Aristotle, Ptolemy); in mathematics (from Euclid, Alhacen, Vitello); in music (from the Psalms, church music); and in theology (from the Bible, church fathers).

In the lengthy work for the doctorate in theology, the most studied works were the Bible and the commentary on the Bible and the church fathers by Peter Lombard. Many other works were consulted and studied by medieval theological scholars including the church fathers and Peter Hispanus' commentary on Aristotle's logic.

The doctor in medicine curriculum was based on the works of Hippocrates, Galen, the medieval encyclopedias of Rhazes and Haly Abbas, the canon of medicine of Avicenna, the materials of Theophilus the Byzantine, the Jewish physician Isaac, and Nicholas of Salerno, and other collected manuscripts written by early physician-teachers. Astrology was an important part of the course at many universities since treatment had to be given in accord with the favorable or unfavorable aspects of the heavens.

The doctor's degree in civil law was based on studies in the Roman law code by Justinian and the commentary on law written by Irnerius. The doctorate in canon law involved the mastering of the compilation of church laws made by Gratian and the books of papal laws added by popes who reigned in the years following the work of Gratian.

Developments in the Degrees

As time progressed a number of changes took place in higher education. There was a marked proliferation of universities in Europe and the British Isles. Universities were established in Scandinavia, Russia, the Americas, the Near and Far East, Australia, New Zealand, India, and Africa. An expansion in degree programs occurred, the emphasis swinging from theological training toward secular pursuits.

The quality of pre-university education improved. Students were more adequately prepared for their doctoral studies.

Educational authorities came to recognize the desirability for the university professor to be a research investigator as well as a teacher. Original work became a part of university training. As new knowledge developed, profound changes were introduced into the subject matter of the various curricula.

All these developments led to changes in the doctoral degrees of the universities. New programs were created leading to new doctorates. The performance of original research became a requirement for almost all doctor's degrees. The total time necessary for the attainment of the doctoral degree was shortened, one or more of the intermediate degrees (bachelor, master, licentiate) being eliminated in many instances. In France, the usual degrees now are licentiate and doctorate, while in Germany only the doctorate is given.

Doctorates in the United States

The first Doctor of Philosophy (Ph.D.) degrees earned in the United States were awarded in 1861 to three persons by Yale University.

The degree was based largely on the German pattern, and required a two-year course of study beyond the bachelor's degree. The course comprised language examinations in Greek and Latin, a thesis presenting the results of an original investigation, and a final examination. Prior to this time, students desiring a Ph.D. had gone to Europe, usually to Germany.

Yale University was followed in awarding the earned

Ph.D. by New York University (1866), University of Pennsylvania (1871), Cornell University (1872), Harvard University (1873), Syracuse University (1873), Columbia University (1875), University of Michigan (1876), Boston University (1877), and Johns Hopkins University (1878). Numerous others followed as graduate education became more available.

Many small liberal arts colleges in the latter part of the nineteenth century awarded "earned" Ph.D. degrees, and the degree was also conferred as an honorary one. After a long struggle, however, only those degrees which had been earned in accordance with the standards of the institutions mentioned above were recognized.

In 1873, when Harvard conferred its first degrees of Ph.D., it also granted an earned Doctor of Science (Sc.D.), the first such degree in the United States. In 1891, New York University awarded the Doctor of Pedagogy (Pd.D.), the degree requirements including advanced courses and a thesis. The first Ph.D. in education was granted by Clark University in 1892. In 1921, the first Doctor of Education degree (Ed.D.) was conferred by Harvard University, the degree having requirements very similar to those introduced for New York University's Pd.D. which the Ed.D. gradually replaced.

The earliest medical schools in the colonies which were to become the United States did not confer a doctorate as a first degree. The original degree was the Bachelor of Medicine (M.B.) or the Bachelor of Physic. This degree was the only earned medical degree awarded before 1770. In conformity with the English system, it was expected that holders of the bachelor's degree would return to school, do graduate study and research, write a thesis, and then receive the advanced research degree of Doctor of Medicine (M.D.).

However, very few returned for the advanced work. Any practitioner of medicine, including those with or without an M.B., came to be accepted by the people as a "doctor." No attention was paid to the distinction between M.B. and M.D. Consequently, the various schools of medicine replaced the M.B. with the M.D., Columbia University awarding the first earned M.D. in 1770. The University of Maryland, in 1848, was the last to make the change.

The first Doctor of Dental Surgery (D.D.S.) degree was awarded in 1841 by the Baltimore College of Dental Surgery. An equivalent degree, the Doctor of Dental Medicine (D.M.D.) was introduced by Harvard in 1869. Several groups other than academic institutions took it upon themselves to "award" medical and dental degrees before the dates of the first academic doctorates.

The first Doctor of Veterinary Medicine (D.V.M.) was given by Cornell University in 1874 to a holder of its Bachelor of Veterinary Medicine (B.V.M.) on the basis of his additional study in Europe. In 1876, the American Veterinary College awarded the first doctorate of this sort earned in the United States, a Doctor of Veterinary Surgery (D.V.S.).

Honorary doctoral degrees have a medieval precedent in the granting of doctorates to various persons by popes. In the thirteenth century, the papacy asserted the right to demand the admittance of any person to the doctorate, regardless of academic qualifications. One of the earliest instances occurred in 1218 when the University of Paris was urged to license a papal favorite. The practice grew considerably in the following centuries. The papal university at Rome also conferred degrees without residence or formal study requirements. The present degree-granting prerogative of the Archbishop of Canterbury stems from this papal activity. Cases are also on record of the emperor awarding such degrees and even delegating the right to other officials.

In 1692, Harvard University awarded the first honorary degree prior to the Revolution, a Doctor of Sacred Theology (S.T.D.). The first honorary M.D. was given by Yale University in 1723, the first honorary Doctor of Laws (LL.D.) by Columbia University in 1769, the first honorary Doctor of Civil Law (D.C.L.) by Columbia University in 1774, and the first honorary Doctor of Divinity (D.D.) by Dartmouth College in 1773.

In 1776, George Washington, who was later awarded several other honorary degrees, received from Harvard University the degree of *Doctor Utriusque Juris, tum Naturae et Gentium, tum Civilis* (Doctor of Both Laws, the Law of Nature and Nations, and the Civil Law). This honorary degree is quite possibly the most comprehensive one ever awarded in America.

The first honorary Doctor of Music (D.Mus.) was conferred by Georgetown University in 1849. In the last half of the nineteenth century the custom of awarding honorary Ph.D. and M.D. degrees grew to scandalous proportions. Determined opposition by academic and medical organizations led to the decrease and finally the demise of this practice.

Several writers have indicated that the University of Piacenza, chartered in 1248, and the University of Ferrara, chartered in 1389, became notorious for selling degrees in a period in their early existence.

In a sense, Piacenza and Ferrara were the predecessors of the commercial degree mills which flourished in the United States during the last century and early in this century. They required only a token scholastic effort, usually entirely by correspondence, plus a substantial fee for a "degree." Included among the offerings were doctorates.

Their "campuses" were usually post office boxes; their faculties consisted of a "president" and a secretary; their catalogs were price lists; their diplomas were worthless. Their degrees were spurious since the schools had absolutely no academic integrity.

One of the earliest degree mills was chartered as Richmond College in 1835. Many of the degrees offered by these counterfeit institutions duplicated legitimate degrees; others were unique to such shady operations. One notorious diploma factory operating in Washington in 1923 offered over sixty-five different degrees. In 1927, the racket was so widespread that a sizeable traffic in United States "doctorates" was being carried on in Europe and other overseas areas. A Berlin newspaper is reported to have carried a cartoon which served as a sharp commentary on the situation. A vending machine was depicted with the inscription: "Put your coin in the slot and pull out an American doctor diploma."

Conclusion

Thus the doctorate can be seen in its many-centuried development. It had humble origins in the title granted to itinerant teachers, who gathered small bands of aspiring learners about them. It has grown into a highly-respected symbol of academic accomplishment and learning in twentieth century society, a symbol of enough renown to encourage counterfeits.

CHAPTER TWO

The Present Status of the Doctorate

doc'tor (dŏk'tẽr), n. fr. OF., fr. L. teacher, fr. docere to teach . . . 2. One who has received the highest degree conferred by a university or college. . . .

— — — WEBSTER'S NEW INTERNATIONAL DICTIONARY.

Types of Degrees

IN THE MODERN United States of America the earned doctorate represents the most advanced degree conferred by a university or college. The title indicates a person who has acquired the highest formal training in his chosen field of learning. Earned doctoral degrees are available today in a wide variety of subjects. The degrees most frequently earned are the Doctor of Philosophy (Ph.D.), the Doctor of Medicine (M.D.), the Doctor of Dental Surgery (D.D.S.), the Doctor of Education (Ed.D.), and the Doctor of Veterinary Medicine (D.V.M.). In recent years, more than 25,000 earned doctorates have been awarded annually, approximately 44 per cent being Ph.D., 30 per cent M.D., 14 per cent D.D.S., 5 per cent Ed.D., 3 per cent D.V.M. The remaining 4 per cent represent over forty other types of doctoral degrees.

When academic degrees were originated, Latin was the language of the educated world. Thus degree designations were written in this tongue. The custom was retained long after the Latin language was abandoned as the medium of teaching in most universities. Many of today's doctorates, although they are named in their English forms, reflect their Latin origins in the abbreviations. For example, one might note: Ph.D. *(Philosophiae Doctor),* M. D. *(Medicinae Doctor),* Sc.D. *(Scientiae Doctor),* Th.D. *(Theologiae Doctor),* and S.J.D. *(Scientiae Juridicae Doctor).* Many of the more recent degrees take the English order of words, as the D.D.S. (Doctor of Dental Surgery) and D.V.M. (Doctor of Veterinary Medicine). However, there is no mandatory form for the abbreviations. Often one degree is abbreviated in two or more ways. The Doctor of Engineering has ten different abbreviation usages, including D.Eng., Eng.D., Dr.Eng., Ing.D. *(Ingenium Doctor),* and E.D.

In general, there are two types of legitimate degrees: earned and honorary. Earned degrees have two categories, research degrees such as the Ph.D. and the Ed.D., and non-research degrees such as the M.D., the D.D.S., and the D.V.M. These categories will be discussed in the following sections.

Earned Research Degrees

The Ph.D. is the conventional mark of the trained scholar who has demonstrated his ability to do original research in one of many fields of endeavor including the arts, the humanities, the biological sciences, the physical sciences, the social sciences, engineering, education, and other areas. In addition the degree has become or is becoming the mark of mature professional preparation for many positions in industry, government, religion, and college and university teaching and research. At present, over 170 schools in the United States offer the Ph.D. in one or more areas of specialization, over 11,000 degrees being awarded each year.

A total of three to five years of study beyond the bachelor's degree is ordinarily spent in the attainment of the Doctor of Philosophy. Sometimes a master's degree is taken along the way, sometimes not. The curriculum usually involves one or two years of advanced course work, qualifying examinations over the basic materials of the field, a comprehensive examination over the specialized area of the field, the demonstration of a reading knowledge of two foreign languages, a research project and a thesis based on it, and a final examination. The research and thesis writing are generally deemed to be the most valuable portion of the doctoral program. Between one and two years is usually spent on this phase.

The names of and brief biographical data on a large number of the persons holding the Ph.D. in the United States may be found in the several-volumed work *American Men of Science* published by The Cattell Press of Tempe, Arizona. These compilations list persons in the biological, physical, social, and behavioral sciences.

The Ed.D. is the only other earned research doctorate that has received extensive recognition. This degree represents professional preparation for positions of leadership in elementary, secondary, and higher education on both the practical and theoretical levels. Original research is considered a necessary part of this preparation. Degrees are awarded in administration, agricultural education, art education, business education, elementary education, educational administration, guidance and counseling, educational psychology, home economics education, health education, higher education, music education, physical education, religious education, science education, speech education, secondary education, and other specialties.

Over ninety U.S. universities offer the Ed.D. and over 1300 degrees are awarded each year. The Doctor of Education usually takes from three to five years of study beyond the bachelor's level. The degree requirements are quite similar to those of the Ph.D. in many schools. A master's degree may or may not be taken as an intermediate step. The Ed.D. program often differs from the curriculum for the Ph.D. in education in that there may be no language requirement, the amount of course work may be greater, and the research and thesis may lean more toward a practical type of study than toward a theoretical one. In numerous cases, however, the distinctions between the two degrees are quite shadowy and in many instances it is impossible to identify which type of degree is involved from the requirements, the thesis topic, or the character of the thesis.

Over twenty educational institutions in the United States offer the earned degree of Doctor of Theology (Th.D.) or Doctor of Sacred Theology (S.T.D.). This doctorate is what might be termed a "long" degree since it has as a prerequisite more than an undergraduate baccalaureate. In addition to the four years of training for the bachelor's degree, three or four years of specialized seminary, theological school, or divinity school training leading to a professional degree are necessary for admission to the doctoral program. This professional degree is usually a Bachelor of Divinity (B.D.) or a Bachelor of Sacred Theology (S.T.B.), or it may be a special ecclesiastical qualification. The curriculum for the doctorate resembles that of the Ph.D. quite closely except that sometimes more than two languages are required.

The Th.D. or S.T.D. is usually sought by persons entering theological teaching and other positions of leadership in religious work. From two to four years beyond the B.D., S.T.B., or ecclesiastical qualification are required for the doctorate, making the total time from undergraduate matriculation nine or more years.

Over forty earned research doctorates in addition to

the Ph.D., Ed.D., Th.D., and S.T.D. are currently being offered by colleges, universities, and specialized schools in the United States. Those given by more than ten institutions include the Doctor of Engineering (D.Eng.), the Doctor of the Science of Law (J.S.D.), the Doctor of Business Administration (D.B.A.), the Doctor of Musical Arts (D.M.A.), the Doctor of Public Health (D.P.H.), and the Doctor of Medical Science (Med. Sc.D.). The degree abbreviations given are the most widely used ones, but there are often other versions. The D.Eng., the D.B.A., and the D.M.A. are similar to the Ph.D. in requirements.

The S.J.D., the D.P.H., and the Med.Sc.D. are, like the Th.D., "long" degrees since they presuppose more than the regular four-year baccalaureate training. The S.J.D. has as a prerequisite the Bachelor of Laws (LL.B.) degree which represents at least six years of college work. The doctorate itself requires an additional two to four years. The D.P.H. and the Med.Sc.D. usually are based on an M.D. or a doctorate in some other medical field (such as a D.D.S. or a D.V.M.) or a doctorate in an allied science (such as a Ph.D. in bacteriology or anatomy). Two to four years are necessary for the completion of the work for these degrees.

The requirements for most of the over forty other doctorates resemble those for the Ph.D., the major emphasis being on an original research project and a thesis. It is of interest to note that the longest research degree awarded in recent years is probably the Doctor of Education in College Teaching in Physical Science, although the Doctor of Science in Petroleum Refining Engineering was a formidable contender. The accompanying chart lists the percentages of the over 13,000 annual research doctorates represented by each of the various fields.

Earned Non-research Degrees

Non-research doctorates, that is, doctor's degrees which do not require a research project and a thesis, are limited almost exclusively to the healing arts and associated fields. The origin of this practice in the United States was traced in the previous chapter where the M.B. was seen to have been elevated to the M.D. The M.D. degree today symbolizes the completion of the basic training necessary for the practice of medicine. It generally does not license a physician to practice; it only certifies his fundamental preparation. It is a degree of integrity and exacting standards resulting from four years of concentrated study, usually following a regular four-year baccalaureate, although some medical schools take entrants after three years of undergraduate preparation.

PERCENTAGE OF ANNUAL RESEARCH DOCTORATES IN VARIOUS FIELDS

Field	%
PHYSICAL SCIENCES	25.7%
Chemistry (11.8%)	
Physics (7.0%)	
Mathematics (3.8%)	
Geology (2.1%)	
Geography (0.6%)	
Astronomy (0.3%)	
EDUCATION	14.6%
ARTS, HUMANITIES	12.7%
Languages, literature (6.2%)	
History (3.3%)	
Religion (1.9%)	
Philosophy (1.3%)	
BEHAVIORAL SCIENCES	11.9%
Psychology (6.7%)	
Political science (2.4%)	
Sociology (2.2%)	
Anthropology (0.6%)	
BIOLOGICAL SCIENCES	11.8%
Zoology, entomology (2.6%)	
Biology, genetics (2.1%)	
Microbiology, bacteriology (1.5%)	
Botany (1.5%)	
Health sciences (1.1%)	
Physiology (1.0%)	
Biochemistry, biophysics (0.9%)	
Pharmacy (0.7%)	
Anatomy (0.4%)	
ENGINEERING	10.2%
BUSINESS	5.8%
Economics (5.1%)	
Food technology (0.3%)	
Business administration (0.3%)	
Journalism (0.1%)	
AGRICULTURE	3.4%
FINE ARTS	3.3%
Speech, theater (1.6%)	
Music (1.4%)	
General (0.3%)	
OTHERS	0.6%
Home economics (0.3%)	
Library science (0.2%)	
Law (0.1%)	

At present, about eighty schools award over 7000 M.D. degrees annually. This is almost one-third of all the doctorates given each year in this country. The four-year curriculum is usually divided almost equally between basic or theoretical studies and clinical or applied work. Included among the studies are anatomy, biochemistry, physiology, pathology, pharmacology, bacteriology, physical diagnosis, laboratory diagnosis, surgery, psychiatry, pediatrics, obstetrics and gynecology, preventive medicine, urology, otolaryngology, ophthamology, and orthopedics.

Every few years a compilation entitled *American Medical Directory* is published by The American Medical Association. This work attempts to list every M.D. practicing in the United States.

Each year over 3000 dentists are graduated by the over forty dental schools of the United States with the degree of D.D.S. or Doctor of Dental Medicine (D.M.D.). The demanding four-year curriculum leading to the doctor's degree has as a prerequisite at least two years of undergraduate college work, although many students enter dental school with more, a sizable number actually holding a bachelor's degree. The modern dental curriculum consists of instruction similar in many ways to that for the M.D., but with emphasis on oral surgery (extractions, removal of cysts, treatment of jaw fractures), operative dentistry (repair of natural teeth), periodontia (treatment of soft tissues around teeth), orthodontia (correction of dental anomalies), and prosthodontia (replacement of lost teeth). As in the case of the M.D., the D.D.S. degree indicates a course of preparation and is not a license to practice the art. Licensing procedures come after the degree is earned.

The volume *American Dental Directory* published by the American Dental Association carries a listing of dentists in the United States.

There are seventeen schools of veterinary medicine in the United States which graduate annually approximately 800 veterinarians with the degree of D.V.M. Two or three years of undergraduate work are prerequisite to enrollment in the rigorous four-year program leading to this degree. The curriculum trains the student in the prevention, cure, alleviation, and extermination of disease among animals, in the nature, causes, and treatment of disorders to which they are subject, and in surgical procedures. The courses resemble those taken by the aspiring physician with the focus switched from the human to the other members of the mammal class.

Doctors of Veterinary Medicine will be found listed in the *Directory of the American Veterinary Association.*

A number of other non-research doctorates are available in a variety of fields in or allied with the healing arts. Two of these are "healing" degrees, which involve the use of drugs and the practice of surgery. The degree of Doctor of Osteopathy (D.O.) is based on a four-year curriculum resembling that for the M.D. Two years of undergraduate college work are required for admission to the five osteopathic schools which graduate about 400 osteopaths each year. None of the osteopathic schools is affiliated with a university. Recently one of the major schools of osteopathy granting the D.O. degree became a school of medicine granting the M.D. The degree of Doctor of Surgical Chiropody (D.S.C.) is awarded by five institutions to about 100 graduates each year. The four-year course is preceded by one or two years of undergraduate college work. These schools train chiropodists or podiatrists who specialize in the diagnosis, prevention, and treatment of foot disorders.

In addition, there are two doctoral degrees which are non-medical in that they do not involve drugs and surgery. One of these is the Doctor of Optometry (O.D.)

which is given by six small specialized institutions and several universities to about 400 graduates annually. The degree is based on one or two years of undergraduate college study plus four years of optometric training. These institutions prepare their graduates to examine vision and to prescribe and dispense optical devices for vision correction.

The Doctor of Chiropractic (D.C.) is awarded by over twelve schools which require a four-year course, and others which seem to demand less. These institutions award degrees to over approximately 500 graduates annually. Chiropractors specialize in the treatment of the nerve system of the body by physiotherapeutic and other mechanical means.

Presented below is a chart of the major earned doctorates granted in the United States. The first column cites the degrees. The second column gives the most widely used abbreviation. The third column shows the degree program in terms of years; the first figure indicates the years of undergraduate preparation; the second figure indicates the years of non-research professional training; and the third figure indicates the years of training leading up to and involving research and a thesis. A split figure like 3/4 is to be read 3 to 4 years. An asterisk indicates that the degree is also given as an honorary one.

Honorary Degrees

Ideally, an honorary doctor's degree awarded by a college or university in the United States should be a highly-deserved recognition of outstanding public service, original creative work, or distinguished endeavor in some field. The degree should signify work corresponding in quality at least to that done for an earned doctorate. Regrettably, practice has often fallen far short of this ideal. Honorary doctorates have been bestowed for publicity purposes, for commercial gain, for political considerations, and for personal vanity and power seeking. Most universities and colleges, however, maintain a high level of integrity in choosing recipients for their honorary doctoral degrees.

MAJOR EARNED DOCTORATES

Doctor of	*Abbrevn.*	*Program*
Business Administration*	D.B.A.	4 - 0 - 3/4
Chiropractic	D.C.	0 - 4
Dental Medicine	D.M.D.	2/3 - 4
Dental Surgery	D.D.S.	2/3 - 4
Education*	Ed.D.	4 - 0 - 3/4
Engineering*	D.Eng.	4/5 - 0 - 3/4
Juridicial Science*	S.J.D.	3 - 3 - 2/4
Medical Science*	Med.Sc.D.	3/4 - 2/4 - 2/3
Medicine	M.D.	3/4 - 4
Music*	D.Mus.	4 - 0 - 3/4
Musical Arts	D.M.A.	4 - 0 - 3/4
Optometry	O.D.	1/2 - 4
Osteopathy	D.O.	2 - 4
Philosophy	Ph.D.	4 - 0 - 3/4
Public Administration*	D.P.A.	4 - 0 - 3/4
Public Health*	D.P.H.	3/4 - 3/4 - 2/3
Religious Education*	D.R.E.	4 - 2 - 2/3
Sacred Music*	S.M.D.	4 - 0 - 4
Sacred Theology*	S.T.D.	4 - 3/4 - 2/3
Science*	Sc.D.	4 - 0 - 3/4
Surgical Chiropody*	D.S.C.	1/2 - 4
Theology	Th.D.	4 - 3/4 - 2/3
Veterinary Medicine	D.V.M.	2/3 - 4

*Given as honorary degree, also.

In recent years, approximately 3000 honorary doctor's degrees have been awarded annually. The most frequently awarded degrees, listed in decreasing order of bestowal and with the most-used abbreviations, are Doctor of Laws (LL.D.),* Doctor of Humane Letters (L.H.D.), Doctor of Divinity (D.D.), Doctor of Science (Sc.D.),* Doctor of Literature (Lit.D.), Doctor of Letters (Litt.D.), Doctor of Music (D.Mus.),* Doctor of Engineering (D.Eng.),* and Doctor of Fine Arts (D.F.A.). Those marked with an asterisk are also awarded as earned degrees.

In addition to these, over sixty other types of honorary doctorates have been awarded in recent times. Among the rare and interesting honorary doctorates which have been granted are the Doctor of Cosmology (D.Co.), the Doctor of Lithuanian Philology (Phil.L.D.), the Doctor of Philanthropy and Charity, and the Doctor of Sanitation (San.D.). The record for honorary doctorates is probably held by former President Herbert Hoover, who has received more than eighty.

Spurious Degrees

In many states, regulations governing the issuance of charters to schools are still quite lax. Supervision of academic quality is often practically non-existent. Thus there remains, in some localities of the United States, the scandal of a number of degree mills or diploma factories. These illegitimate operations sell spurious degrees at a price to unwary or unscrupulous customers. Two types of spurious doctorates are peddled, those purporting to be legitimate degrees and carrying either the same designations or the same abbreviations (or both) as authentic degrees, and those with unique designations not duplicating degrees of legitimate schools.

Prices for spurious doctorates usually range in the region of several hundred dollars, those duplicating legitimate degrees commanding the higher prices. Some operators even offer to create a degree of any title for an appropriate fee. As one might expect, the majority of spurious doctorates carry designations implying them to be in the healing arts, religion, and psychology. A few of the more interesting ones are the Doctor of Biopsychology, the Doctor of Divinity in Biopsychodynamic Religions, the Doctor of Eclectic, the Doctor of Psychotherapy, the Doctor of Spiritual Divinity, the Doctor of Universal Truth, and the Doctor of Character Analysis.

Doctorates of Other Countries

When one takes a world-wide view of earned doctoral degrees, the major factor that is noted is the tendency in many countries to award the doctorate only on the basis of research and a thesis. This is particularly exemplified in the medical sciences. In many countries it is not necessary to hold a doctor's degree in order to practice medicine, dentistry, and veterinary medicine. At the termination of the four to seven year training period, some sort of professional title or a degree other than the doctorate is awarded.

For example, in most nations of the British Commonwealth and in some others, the joint degrees of Bachelor of Medicine and Bachelor of Surgery (M.B., Ch.B.) are awarded in medicine, the degree of bachelor of Dental Surgery (B.D.S.) in dentistry, and the Degree of Bachelor of Veterinary Science (B.V.S.) in that field. These degrees are quite sufficient to justify practice in the healing arts since the training they represent is very similar to that for which a doctorate is awarded in the United States.

To persons who choose to earn doctorates in these fields, further study involving research and a thesis may be pursued. However, most medical, dental, and veterinary practitioners do not take this further step.

In the U.S.S.R. medical practice is based on the professional Diploma Vrač, in some South American countries on the professional title of Medico-Cirujano, in Czechoslovakia on the title Promovany Lekar, in Denmark and Norway on the degree of Candidatus Medicinae, in Japan on the Igakushi degree, in Poland on the professional Diploma Lekarz, in Spain on the Licenciado, and in Sweden on the Licentiat. In most of these countries, if a physician desires to do further study involving research and a thesis, a doctorate may be earned. The situations are quite similar for the professions of dentistry and of veterinary medicine.

There is a remarkable variety in the degree programs leading to the doctor's degree in different countries. The total time required for the doctorate is from five to seven years after the completion of secondary education (high school).

In Germany, Austria, and Italy a student proceeds directly to the the doctorate, there being no intermediate steps or degrees.

In other countries, the aspiring doctoral scholar goes through one or more intermediate degrees or stages of qualification. In most cases, there is one intermediate stage which may be variously named. For example, bachelor is used in the British Commonwealth and licentiate or some professional title in many South American and Central and South European countries. In some nations, there are two intervening steps. In Bulgaria, Czechoslovakia, Rumania, and the U.S.S.R., these are the professional title or specialist and the candidate; in Japan they are the gakushi (bachelor) and shushi (master); in The Netherlands they are the candidate and the doctorandus; and in Finland and Sweden they are the candidate and the licentiate.

Some educational systems offer what might be termed higher doctorates. In most of the universities of the British Commonwealth, a Ph.D. can be taken by devoting two to three years beyond the undergraduate level to supervised research and thesis preparation. In addition to the Ph.D., however, there are the higher or senior doctorates, including the D.Litt., D.Mus., D.Sc., LL.D., D.Soc.Sci., and M.D. These doctor's degrees are awarded on the basis of substantial published contributions to knowledge which are submitted to the university.

In the U.S.S.R. and some of the countries on its borders the only type of doctorate is the so-called higher one. The complete pattern of this degree includes these procedures:

After five or six years of study, the student receives a Specialist diploma or a professional title. Another three to five years of study including the thesis yields the Candidate degree, which is equivalent to the Ph.D. in the character of the attainment. Then, after substantial contributions to the knowledge of a given field and submission of these materials to a university, the doctorate is awarded. The doctor's degree thus comes some years after formal training at the university has been completed. The degree often serves as part of the qualifications for a university teaching post.

In Germany, Poland, Belgium, and a few other nations additional research work after the doctorate leads to the university teaching qualification which often takes the form of a higher doctorate.

Among the more interesting facets of the doctorates of other countries are the degree designations. Some nations give only a few doctorates; other have proliferated the degree signatures considerably.

In the German-speaking countries, among the degrees found are Dr.agr. (agriculture), Dr.rer.hort. (horticulture), Dr.ing. (engineering), Dr.iur. (law), Dr.med. (medicine), Dr.med.dent. (dentistry), Dr.med.vet. (veterinary medicine), Dr.mont. (mining), Dr.phil. (philosophy), Dr.rer.nat. (natural science), Dr.rer.oec. (economics), Dr.rer.pol. (political science), Dr.techn. (technology), and Dr. theol. (theology).

In France, the most used degrees are Doctorat en Droit (law), Doctorat en Science Politique, Doctorat ès Sciences Economiques, Doctorat en Medicin, Doctorat en Pharmacie, Doctorat ès Sciences, Doctorat ès Lettres, and Doctorat de l'Universite (the latter for foreign students), plus the Diplôme d'Ingenieur-Docteur. In Italy, all doctorates are known as Laurea.

Japanese doctor's degrees read -hakushi, and thus one

finds designations such as Hogakuhakushi (law), Kogaku-hakushi (technology), Igakuhakushi (medicine), Rigaku-hakushi (science), Kyoikugakuhakushi (education), and Suisangakuhakushi (fishery science). In the USSR, essentially the only designation in use is Doktor nauk (sciences).

Conclusion

And so the doctorate is seen in its many-faceted present day manifestations. The variations in type, in program, and in designations present an interesting array. The holder of a doctorate gets the feeling that he is part of a much larger intellectual community, a community of persons with the title "Doctor" which knows no national boundaries.

CHAPTER THREE

The Etiquette of the Doctorate

Tell me once more what title thou dost bear.
——— W. SHAKESPEARE, *The Merchant of Venice*..

Degrees are taken to be used. The degree or title becomes a part of one's name, and should be used just as much, and serves just as much to identify a person, as his christian name. In writing to a stranger, it indicates your attainments, and is a better introduction to him than a whole letter of explanation.
——— F. S. THOMAS, 1887

Basic Considerations

FAIRLY WIDESPREAD uncertainty is evident among many persons concerning the professional and social uses of the doctoral degrees, the degree abbreviations, and the title Doctor. In order to attempt at least a partial resolution of the problem, the writer of this handbook has consulted a considerable variety of source materials. These include numerous etiquette and social usage books, secretarial handbooks, magazine articles, statements made by professional societies having memberships totally or in part made up of doctorate holders, and editorials and letters in professional journals. In addition, letters have been written to executive secretaries of professional organizations, surveys of leading radio, television, newspaper, magazine, and journal usage have been conducted, inquiries have been directed to the cultural attaches of embassies of foreign countries, and a poll of a considerable number of persons having doctorates of the five major types (Ph.D., M.D., D.D.S., Ed.D., and D.V.M.) has been conducted. Although there was considerable divergence in detailed opinions, the data gathered from all these sources revealed a general concensus, by considerably more than a majority, which warrants some broad general conclusions.

1. The first conclusion to be recognized is that all holders of a legitimately earned doctoral degree have an equal right to the usage of the title Doctor. A legitimate doctoral degree may be defined as one requiring six or more years of training in an established, reputable school in the United States, or an equivalent doctorate from a foreign country. It is never incorrect to address any holder of such a degree as Doctor, unless he indicates that he personally prefers not to be. The term doctor is to be regarded as generic rather than specific. It refers to any individual who holds a doctoral degree and thus should not be synonymous with the possessor of any one type or any restricted class of doctorates. As both the history and the derivation of the term indicate, the basic meaning of the word doctor implies a person learned in a given field, that is, it denotes an expert by virtue of a background of rigorous training sufficient to qualify him to teach the subject.

2. The second conclusion is that there exists confusion in a number of circles about the term doctor as a synonym for physician and the term Doctor as a title of address for holders of all doctorates.

The historical origins of this ambiguity are quite well known. Medieval universities awarded doctorates in many fields. The holders of university doctoral degrees in medicine emphasized that they were Doctors in order to distinguish themselves from charlatans and non-university trained physicians. There were more in the latter two categories in many lands for many centuries. The untrained practitioners saw the utility of the title Doctor and so they applied it also to themselves. In addition, most of the people generally did not discern the difference and applied the title uncritically to all medical practitioners. Although the title Doctor was used in the Middle Ages by holders of doctorates in other fields, some did not have as much contact with the people as did Doctors of medicine. A good example would be university teachers. In other cases, different titles took precedence. Ecclesiastical titles often were used by clerics in preference to their doctoral titles. Thus arose the confusion of doctor as a specific professional designation and Doctor as a general title.

If one takes an international view, the term physician comes closest to being a common title by which practically all members of the medical profession can be identified throughout the world. There is fairly general agreement in many circles that the term physician would be a better one to use than the imprecise doctor when one is referring to a person as a practitioner of medicine, with the term Doctor being reserved as a title for all holders of doctor's degrees, physicians included. This is seen to be even more reasonable when it is recognized that in many places all physicians may not hold doctorates.

3. The third conclusion that can be derived from the survey is a general rule of thumb which can serve as an approximate guide to the usage of the title Doctor. This rule, which will be the basis for further discussion in this chapter, may be stated as follows:

If the expertise represented by a doctoral degree is pertinent to the situation, then the title should be used, unless the holder of the degree prefers otherwise.

If the expertise is not pertinent, the title may or may

not be used, depending upon personal preference, local custom, and the degree of separation between the social and professional life of the possessor of the doctorate.

This is not meant to be a hard, fast rule, but to be recognized as a reflection of general opinion as to how the title of Doctor should be handled in most instances. Individual choice is important, and this should be taken into account, especially with regard to social usage. Some modifications of this general outlook will be presented in later sections dealing with specific professions and specific doctorates.

It is most certainly advisable to handle the title Doctor with discretion. One should avoid the extremes of pretension and ostentation. On the other hand, one should avoid the opposite extreme of an overly-apologetic, falsely-humble, or pseudo-sophisticated reluctance to use the title or to indicate that one is the holder of a doctorate. This tension is not always successfully maintained, and different persons will handle it differently. As long, however, as one acts in a friendly, considerate, and not overly-sensitive manner, and keeps his sense of humor, good taste can be served.

In general, honorary degrees are not treated as are earned ones. Most holders of these degrees who do not also hold earned doctorates are not addressed either professionally or socially as Doctor. The major exceptions to this are persons in the religious professions, and usually college and university professors. Under no circumstances are purchasers of spurious degrees to be accorded the title Doctor.

In the sections to follow, the various professions employing doctoral degree holders will be treated. Under each, the professional use of the degree and the title will be discussed, then the private use will be treated. The basic rule of thumb will be applied with a fair degree of consistency, with allowance being made for differences in individual group preferences.

Each section is intended to be complete in itself. Some repetition will be encountered by those who read the remainder of this chapter continuously. This arrangement was deemed advisable since it permits ready reference to the etiquette in a given profession.

The Medical Profession

Professional Usage

Practically every physician in the United States holds an M.D. degree. When the possessor of this degree sets himself up in practice and makes his services available to the public, the M.D. certifies to his prospective patients his basic preparation and thus his expertise in the area of medicine. Since the degree is pertinent to his professional activity, he may employ the degree designation following his name

JOHN R. COE, M.D.

and he may utilize the title Doctor, which is usually abbreviated Dr.

DR. JOHN R. COE

In his professional life, he is addressed as Dr. Coe by all persons who come into contact with him, including his patients, his colleagues, and auxiliary medical personnel. If there is any doubt that others know him to be an M.D., he may refer to himself as Doctor, although he usually calls himself John Doe, since most persons will know of his degree by virtue of the professional situation. If he has occasion to speak of other persons who have doctorates (D.D.S., D.V.M., Ph.D., Ed.D., Th.D.), he addresses them with the title, adding some modifying phrase to indicate the type of doctorate involved. For example, he may refer to Dr. Doe, a dentist, Dr. Noe, a veterinarian, Dr. Poe, a university botany professor, Dr. Roe, the superintendent of schools, and Dr. Yoe, the minister of his church.

When John R. Coe, M.D. is mentioned in the news media (newspapers, news magazines, radio, television) in relation to his professional activities, he is referred to as Dr. John R. Coe, with some indication being given that his doctorate is in medicine. When he appears as a speaker in a situation where his medical expertise is pertinent, he is presented as Dr. John R. Coe and the details of his introduction will make it plain that he is a physician. On articles and books which he has written, his name ordinarily appears as John R. Coe, M.D. with brief biographical details being added in an accompanying note or footnote.

On the rolls of organizations of which he is a member or patron, his name is given as John R. Coe, M.D. In the telephone directory his listing is presented as Coe John R MD or Coe John R phys or as Coe John R if it appears under a general heading of physicians. When his name is listed under a general heading, his area of practice and office hours usually accompany it. The Doctor of Medicine's outdoor office sign, his office door sign, and his desk marker will generally take the form of his name followed by M.D. plus a designation of his area of practice on the second line. An example would appear as follows.

JOHN R. COE, M.D.
Radiology

On letterheads, statements, prescription blanks, envelope return addresses, business cards, appointment cards, and printed checks for a professional account, the physician's name appears as John R. Coe, M.D. with the addition of the area of practice, the detailed address, and any other necessary items. When signing a letter, the physician affixes his name as *John R. Coe* if he is signing a printed letterhead or form which shows his M.D.; otherwise he signs *John R. Coe* over the typewritten words John R. Coe, M.D. or just *John R. Coe, M.D.* The M.D. should appear only once on the letter or form.

When persons write to a physician both the envelope and inside addresses should be written as Dr. John R. Coe or John R. Coe, M.D. with the further details of address added. Neither Dr. John R. Coe, M.D. nor Mr. John R. Coe, M.D. is good form. The salutation of a letter written to a physician generally takes the form Dear Dr. Coe, although Dear Sir is also proper.

For a woman physician, the above conventions apply to Dr. Mary J. Coe. If she is married the last name may be either her husband's last name or her maiden name. She is not addressed as Miss or Mrs. in her professional work, but as Doctor at all times.

Osteopathic physicians (D.O.) and podiatrists (D.S.C.) follow about the same professional etiquette as do those who hold M.D. degrees. It should be made plain in all use of the title Doctor exactly what type of doctorate it is that is being referred to.

Private Usage

For most physicians whose professional service is available to the public, there is considerable overlap between their professional and their private lives. In addition, the expertise of many physicians is likely to be of pertinence in practically any situation with regard to medical emergencies. Also, most of a medical man's personal friends will know him to be a possessor of a doctorate. Thus the practitioner of medicine is almost always addressed as Doctor in private life.

In general, a physician will not introduce himself in

private life as Dr. Coe, but as John Coe. When he is subsequently asked what occupation he follows, as generally occurs, and answers that he is a physician, his newly-made acquaintances will then address him as Doctor.

Socially the title is not to be made evident by the physician himself to other people; it is to be found out or allowed to emerge in the context of the situation. When other persons, however, introduce the physician, they should call him Dr. Coe and then add a phrase explaining that he is a physician, a medical man, a psychiatrist, or some other term indicating directly or indirectly the type of doctorate he holds.

With relation to mail he receives at home, to tradesmen, to banking personnel, and to other commercial people, the physician may or may not choose to employ his title of Doctor. The most widespread practice is for him to do so, and thus he gives his name as Dr. John R. Coe. It may appear thus or as John R. Coe, M.D. on credit cards. If patients may need to find him at home, if he is willing to be called on in emergencies, or if his office is in conjunction with his home, his mail box or house marker may read John R. Coe, M.D. Otherwise, it should read John R. Coe.

Written or engraved formal invitations, acceptances, regrets, and announcements will usually employ the title Doctor. A physician's engraved social name card or that of himself and his wife will read Dr. John Robert Coe or Dr. and Mrs. John Robert Coe. In dispatching informal notes, letters, and greetings (such as Christmas cards) the physician signs only his name, since these go out to acquaintances who are familiar with the writer and his title.

A few physicians prefer to be Mister in private life. A number of others assume this status when out of their communities on non-professional activities (such as a vacation). The title Mister in such cases permits a professional anonymity which results in an often sought-after privacy. Many married women physicians prefer to be known in private life as Mrs. John R. Coe rather than as Dr. Mary J. Coe; others do not. Unmarried women physicians generally carry the title Doctor over into their private lives, although a number use Miss.

Osteopathic physicians (D.O.) and podiatrists (D.S.C.) follow the private usage custom of Doctors of Medicine. Degree distinctions should be made clear so that there is no confusion with holders of M.D. degrees.

The Dental Profession

Professional Usage

The degree of D.D.S. or D.M.D. is held by almost every practitioner of dentistry in the United States. Either of these equivalent doctoral degrees indicates to those who seek dental care that the degree holder has expertise in this area. Since the degree is thus pertinent to his professional work, the dentist may employ the degree designation following his name

JAMES L. DOE, D.D.S.

and the title Doctor, abbreviated Dr., may be applied.

DR. JAMES L. DOE

In his professional activities, his associates, his assistants, and his patients address him as Dr. Doe, and he similarly refers to other dentists. He may refer to himself as Dr. Doe or as James Doe, the former being used if there is any doubt as to how he is to be addressed. In making mention of other persons possessing doctorates (M.D., D.V.M., Ph.D., Ed.D., Th.D.), he uses the title Doctor in conjunction with their last names, adding some information revealing the type of degrees they have.

In newspapers, news magazines, on radio and television, the dentist is called Dr. James L. Doe with some phrase being added to indicate that he holds a dental doctorate. As a speaker from a public platform on a subject in which his expertise is relevant, he is presented as Dr. James L. Doe, a dentist. On articles and books authored by him, the dentist's name is given as James L. Doe, D.D.S.

The name of a dental practitioner on rolls of an organization takes the form James L. Doe, D.D.S. In the telephone directory listing, the name may appear as Doe James L DDS or Doe James L dent or Doe James L when his name appears under the classified heading dentists. In the latter case, specialties and office hours are often added. For his outdoor office sign, office door sign, and desk marker, the dentist uses his name followed by D.D.S. (or D.M.D.) plus the term Dentist or the designation of his area of specialization.

JAMES L. DOE, D.D.S.
Dentist

The name with D.D.S. suffixed, the term Dentist or the area of specialization, the detailed address and any other pertinent items are used on letterheads, statements, prescription blanks, envelope return addresses, business cards, appointment cards, and printed checks for a professional account. If the degree designation is printed on a letter or a form, the signature is *James L. Doe,* if not, the signature will be *James L. Doe, D.D.S.* or *James L. Doe* signed over the typewritten James L. Doe, D.D.S.

When writing to a dentist, both the envelope and inside addresses are written as Dr. James L. Doe or James L. Doe, D.D.S. with the other particulars of the address added. Neither of the forms Dr. James L. Doe, D.D.S. or Mr. James L. Doe, D.D.S. is correct. The salutation of a letter addressed to a dentist appears as Dear Dr. Doe or as Dear Sir.

Private Usage

Since their services are made available to the general public, there is often a large amount of interlocking between the professional and private or social activities of most dentists, especially in small or moderate-sized communities. Most of the social acquaintances of a dentist will have knowledge of his profession and therefore of his degree. Hence, dentists are usually addressed as Doctor in private life as well as in professional.

The dentist does not customarily introduce himself as Dr. Doe, but as James Doe. Almost always newly-made acquaintances will quickly discover him to be a dentist and will henceforth call him Dr. Doe. The title in such circumstances is allowed to develop indirectly out of the relationship. When other persons introduce the dentist to new acquaintances, they should address him as Dr. Doe and then identify him as a dentist to distinguish him from other holders of doctorates.

With regard to mail that comes to his home address and to dealings with tradespersons, service personnel, and banking people, the dentist may employ his title of Doctor or not as he desires. It is the most usual custom for him to do so, and he therefore gives them his name as Dr. James L. Doe. On credit cards he may have his name written in this fashion or as James L. Doe, D.D.S. If patients may need to find him in an emergency, or if his office is at his home, his mail box or house marker may read James L. Doe, D.D.S. Otherwise, the degree designation is omitted.

When he or his wife sends out written or engraved formal invitations, acceptances, regrets, and announcements, the title Doctor may be employed. Likewise his or his and his wife's engraved social card will read Dr. James Langly Doe. He does not use his title or degree abbreviation when he writes informal notes, letters, and greetings (like Christmas cards) ; he signs only James L. Doe or on occasion only his first name.

A few dentists whose life patterns show a sharp separation between professional and private activities prefer to be Mister in the latter. Others assume such a role when on vacation for the sake of privacy.

The Veterinary Medical Profession

Professional Usage

To practice veterinary medicine in the United States, the veterinarian almost without exception must hold the degree of D.V.M., or V.M.D. as it is sometimes styled. In this degree, persons who call upon the veterinarian for his services see a mark of his competency as evidenced by his background of training. Since the degree symbolizes his expertise, in his professional work he may write the degree initials after his name

ERIC G. NOE, D.V.M.

and may use the doctoral title before it.

DR. ERIC G. NOE

In all of his professional relationships he is addressed as Dr. Noe. He may refer to himself and to other members of his profession with the title, and his associates, his assistants, and those who retain his services will so address him. In many cases, especially where it is known that his proper title is Doctor, he will refer to himself as Eric Noe instead of Dr. Noe. In recognition of the character of the doctoral degree, he refers to all holders of other doctorates (M.D.,

D.D.S., Ph.D., Ed.D., Th.D.) as Doctor, usually adding some statement to indicate the kind of degree.

In the various news media (newspapers, news magazines, radio, television), Eric G. Noe, D.V.M. is called Dr. Eric G. Noe with some indication that he is a veterinarian being included. If and when he has occasion to do public speaking on a subject related to his expertise, he is presented to his audience as Dr. Eric G. Noe with added remarks to make it clear that he is a Doctor of Veterinary Medicine. When he writes technical articles or books, his name appears on them as Eric G. Noe, D.V.M.

On lists of members of organizations his listing reads Eric G. Noe, D.V.M. In the telephone directory his name will appear as Noe Eric G DVM or Noe Eric G vet; when his name comes under the general heading of veterinarians in the classified section, it may be listed as Noe Eric G. The area of specialty and office hours may be included in the latter type of listing. The outdoor office sign, the office door sign, and the desk marker of the Doctor of Veterinary Medicine will show his name followed by his degree plus the term Veterinarian.

ERIC G. NOE, D.V.M.
Veterinarian

In some cases an area of specialized practice may be added to or substituted for the term Veterinarian.

On letterheads, statements, envelope return addresses, business cards, appointment cards, and printed checks for a professional account will appear the name with D.V.M. added, the term Veterinarian or the area of specialization, the address, and any other needed items. The veterinarian's signature when the printed letterhead has his D.V.M. on it appears as *Eric G. Noe;* otherwise it appears as *Eric G. Noe* signed above the typewritten Eric G. Noe, D.V.M. or as *Eric G. Noe, D.V.M.*

When letters are sent to a veterinarian by other persons, both the inside and envelope addresses are written as Dr. Eric G. Noe plus the further items of the complete address. Alternately, the letter may be addressed to him as Eric G. Noe, D.V.M. Both Dr. Eric G. Noe, D.V.M. and Mr. Eric G. Noe, D.V.M. are in poor taste. The salutation of a letter to a veterinarian reads Dear Dr. Noe or Dear Sir.

Private Usage

As is the case with the majority of physicians and dentists, a veterinarian's circle of friends in private life will probably include persons related to him professionally. Those who are not will know of his doctoral degree, and thus in most cases there is carryover of the title. The veterinarian is thus usually addressed as Doctor in private life as well as in his professional activities.

He generally does not introduce himself socially as Dr. Noe but as Eric Noe. When his newly-made acquaintances discover him to be a veterinarian, they will thereafter address him as Doctor. When others introduce him they should refer to him as Dr. Noe, adding that his vocation is veterinary medicine.

Most veterinarians have the mail sent to their private residences addressed to them as Doctor and they are thus known by business people in their communities. His name may appear as Dr. Eric G. Noe or as Eric G. Noe, D.V.M. on credit cards and bank accounts, or he may choose to use only Eric G. Noe. If the veterinarian's office is at his place of residence, or if he may be called upon at his home in case of emergency, his home mail box or house marker may read Eric G. Noe, D.V.M. If not, the degree should be omitted.

When the veterinarian sends out informal notes, letters, and greetings (such as Christmas cards) he uses neither his title nor his degree initials. When he sends formal written or engraved invitations, acceptances, regrets, and announcements he may use his doctoral title. If he chooses, his social name card can read Dr. Eric Gregory Noe and that of him and his wife Dr. and Mrs. Eric Gregory Noe.

Some veterinarians prefer to be Mister in private and social life or when they are away from the locale of their practice on vacations or other non-professional activities. This allows them to be purely private citizens at times when they deem this desirable.

The Teaching Profession

Professional Usage

Many college and university teachers, research workers, and administrators, as well as some primary and secondary teachers and administrators, are holders of doctoral degrees. Many fields of specialization are involved. Practically every type of doctorate is represented Ph.D., Ed.D., M.D., D.D.S., D.V.M., and others. These degrees certify to those who utilize the services of such educators that the degree holders have made the maximum formal preparation for their positions. Since the expertises represented by these degrees are therefore pertinent to the professional situations, the holder of a doctorate who is engaged in primary, secondary, or higher education as a teacher, research worker, or administrator may write his degree initials after his name

DALE B. POE, Ph.D.

and may employ the doctoral title preceding it.

DR. DALE B. POE

In the large majority of educational institutions, the doctoral-holding teacher, researcher, or administrator is addressed by his associates, auxiliary school personnel, students, and all others who come into professional contact with him as Dr. Poe. There are, however, a few academic communities, some groups, and some individuals who prefer not to employ the title Doctor or else do not use it consistently. They sometimes use the title Professor or the title Mister as a substitute, as taking precedence, or as interchangeable. By far the most widespread practice conforms to the basic rule, with the doctoral title being employed consistently for all doctorate holders. Dale B. Poe, Ph.D. (or Ed.D., M.D., D.D.S., D.V.M.) in his profession of education may refer to himself as Dr. Poe when introducing himself to students or when making himself known to auxiliary school personnel. Alternately, if he chooses, he may use the title Professor if he holds it, or he may simply call himself Dale Poe, the latter quite often being his way of identifying himself to his colleagues. Ordinarily he uses the title Doctor when referring to associates who hold a doctor's degree, as they do toward him, and he also addresses doctoral-holding persons outside the school circles as Doctor (physicians, dentists, veterinarians, research scientists, psychologists).

When Dale B. Poe, Ph.D. is referred to over the radio or television or in the newspaper or a news magazine in reference to his professional work, the title Doctor is employed with an appended statement indicating his position, specialty, and usually his school. When making public addresses relating to his expertise, he is introduced as Dr. Dale B. Poe and his position and area of concentration are made clear. In professional journal articles and books, his name appears as Dale B. Poe or as Dale B. Poe, Ph.D. with his professional connection and details of his educational biography including the doctorate often being added in a footnote or some other appropriate place. In popular articles, the form used is Dale B. Poe, Ph.D. with a footnote giving his position, school, and educational background in brief.

On rolls of organizations with which he is associated, his name may be carried as Dr. Dale B. Poe, Prof. Dale B. Poe (if he has the title), or Dale B. Poe, depending on the organization's custom and his personal preference. His name appears in the telephone directory as Poe Dale B. Office door signs of doctoral degree holders in most schools carry only his name, as do building directories. Desk markers may take several forms, two possible variations being shown below.

DALE B. POE, PH.D.
Professor of Psychology
DALE B. POE
Ph.D. (Psychology)

Other appropriate degrees (Ed.D., M.D., D.D.S., D.V.M., etc.) may be substituted for Ph.D., other appropriate designations for Professor of Psychology, and other appropriate fields for Psychology.

On letterheads, the name with Ph.D. (or other appropriate degree initials) added, plus the position (Professor of Botany, Dean of the Faculty of Philosophy, Research Associate in Economics) usually appears below and to the left of the departmental name, institutional name, and address, the latter three being centered at the top. On business cards, either Dale B. Poe, Ph.D. or Dr. Dale B. Poe, the position designation, the school, the address, and any other pertinent items may appear. In signing letters the educator writes *Dale B. Poe*. If the name, degree, and position do not appear on the letterhead, he may sign over the typewritten Dale B. Poe, Ph.D. or Dale B. Poe plus the designation of his position. His return address usually appears as Dr. Dale B. Poe or Dale B. Poe, Ph.D. plus his position or department, his school, and its address.

When correspondence is dispatched to him, both the inside and envelope addresses read Dr. Dale B. Poe or Dale B. Poe, Ph.D. plus his position or department, his school, and the address. Often it is not known whether an educator holds a doctorate. In most universities and in many colleges sizable fractions of the faculty on the professional level hold doctorates. This is especially true in the arts and sciences and in departments offering graduate training. However, if there is reasonable doubt, the educator may be addressed by a known title (Professor, Dean, President), as Mister, or without any title as Dale B. Poe. The proper salutation of a letter to an educator with a doctorate is Dear Dr. Poe or if there is doubt about the degree, Dear Sir.

In professional circles a woman educator ordinarily uses her first and middle names (or initial) coupled with her husband's or her maiden last name. In all respects she handles her doctorate as do men. Holders of other doctorates who are engaged in the teaching profession use the degrees as indicated above with the proper substitution in the examples.

Private Usage

The services of educators in this country are in a large sense available to the populace in general. There is usually considerable interconnection between the professional and private lives of many educators. Thus the title of most doctorate holding educators usually carries over, and they are addressed in private life by their friends as Doctor.

The educator with a doctor's degree does not introduce himself socially with the title, but presents himself as Dale Poe. His doctoral status is allowed to develop in the conversation, but if it does not, this should not be considered of great moment. When his acquaintances introduce him to others, they generally call him Dr. Poe, unless he asks them not to do so. Some words are ordinarily added in order to make clear what his professional position is and thus what type of doctorate his is.

With regard to mail he receives at home, some educators use the title, others do not; most receive mail addressed in a variety of ways. In relationships with tradespeople and other community business personnel, he ordinarily does not make a point of the title, but he may use it if he wishes. Those who know him personally or know of his doctorate otherwise will usually address him as Doctor. He may use his title on charge accounts, credit cards, and bank accounts or not, as he desires. His mail box reads Dale B. Poe.

A number of educators, especially ones with separated professional and private lives, choose not to use the title Doctor in their private associations. In most cases the educator who holds a doctorate will find himself comfortable in his social life being addressed as both Doctor and Mister (with Professor often mixed in), the predominating form depending on his personal desires, the divergence between his professional and private activities, other persons involved, and the nature of the situation. Written or engraved formal invitations, acceptances, regrets, and announcements may employ his doctoral title if he wishes, and social cards will read Dr. Dale Bentley Poe or Dr. and Mrs. Dale Bentley Poe. Informal and personal communications employ neither his title nor his degree designation, since they ordinarily are sent to close friends.

The Religious Profession

Professional Usage

Many persons engaged in the religious profession are holders of doctoral degrees. Members of the clergy may possess the earned degrees Th.D., S.T.D., Ph.D., or D.H.L. (Doctor of Hebrew Literature) or the honorary degrees D.D., S.T.D., LL.D., or D.H.Litt. (Doctor of Hebrew Letters) or others. Directors of music in religious institutions may hold degrees of S.M.D., D.Mus., D.M.A., or Ph.D. and directors of religious education may possess an Ed.D., D.R.E., or Ph.D. degree. In addition, many professors in theological schools and some non-ordained officials have doctorates. Persons who are not ordained members of the clergy handle their doctorates in a fashion similar to that for those in the teaching profession. Forms of address for the clergy vary in the several denominations. For this reason, a separate treatment will be given to each of the major variations.

In the Roman Catholic Church, the title Doctor is rarely used either in spoken or written form. It is superseded by ecclesiastical titles for practically every member of the clergy. About the only use made of the doctoral designation is that the initials of the degree may be suffixed to the name of the degree holder in its written form. A Roman Catholic priest who holds a doctorate is addressed as Father Yoe, and is introduced as The Reverend Father Yoe or as Father Yoe. In the news media, he is referred to as The Reverend Albert S. Yoe and Father Yoe. His name appears on organizational rolls, printed stationery, business cards, and a desk marker as The Reverend Albert S. Yoe, S.T.D. The initials of his religious order or society may be added or substituted for the S.T.D. His position is generally added on stationery, cards, and the desk marker. In the telephone directory his listing appears as Yoe Albert S Rev. He is addressed in writing as The Reverend Albert S. Yoe, S.T.D., with Reverend Father as a formal salutation or Dear Father Yoe as an informal one. Appendix 3 provides a listing of forms of address for the higher clergy.

In the Protestant Episcopal Church, the title Doctor is quite frequently employed for priests but not as frequently for the higher clergy. An Episcopal priest who has a doctor's degree may be addressed as Dr. Yoe or as Father Yoe, the latter being preferred in high church. Introductions usually employ the forms The Reverend Dr. Yoe or Father Yoe. In the news media, he is mentioned as The Reverend Dr. Albert S. Yoe and Dr. Yoe or Father Yoe. His name may be placed on organizational rolls, printed stationery, business cards, and a desk marker as The Reverend Albert S. Yoe, Th.D. or The Reverend Dr. Albert S. Yoe. His position is usually included on stationery, cards, and a marker. He signs letters as *Albert S. Yoe* with The Reverend Albert S. Yoe, Th.D. typewritten beneath if it does not appear on the stationery. In the telephone directory his listing is Yoe Albert S Rev. Letters to him are addressed to The Reverend Dr. Albert S. Yoe or the Reverend Albert S. Yoe, Th.D., with Reverend Sir as a formal salutation and Dear Dr. Yoe as an informal one. Appendix 4 gives the proper forms of address for higher Episcopal clergy.

In practically all denominations a Protestant clergyman with a doctor's degree is addressed as Dr. Yoe. Introductions may use either The Reverend Dr. Yoe or Dr. Yoe, phrases being added in the latter case to make it known that he is a member of the clergy. In the news media, he is referred to as The Reverend Dr. Albert S. Yoe and Dr. Yoe. On organizational rolls, printed stationery, business cards, and a desk marker, his name appears as The Reverend Albert S. Yoe, Th.D. or The Reverend Dr. Albert S.

Yoe with his official position added in most instances. He affixes his signature of *Albert S. Yoe* to letters over the typewritten The Reverend Albert S. Yoe, Th.D. unless this appears elsewhere on the stationery. In the telephone directory he is listed as Yoe Albert S Rev or as Yoe Albert S min. Letters to him are addressed to The Reverend Dr. Albert S. Yoe or to The Reverend Albert S. Yoe, Th.D., the salutation being Dear Dr. Yoe. The main exception to these general Protestant forms is the case of the Methodist bishop, where the title Bishop usually supersedes that of Doctor.

A Jewish rabbi with a doctorate is addressed and introduced as Dr. Yoe or as Rabbi Yoe, added information being supplied in the former case to indicate him to be a rabbi. In the news media, he is called Dr. Abraham S. Yoe and Dr. Yoe. His name appears on organizational rolls, business cards, printed stationery, and a desk marker as Rabbi Abraham S. Yoe, Ph.D. or as Dr. Abraham S. Yoe with his position added. He signs letters as *Abraham S. Yoe* placed over the typewritten words Rabbi Abraham S. Yoe, Ph.D. unless the latter is shown on the stationery. His name is given in the telephone directory as Yoe Abraham S Rabbi. Correspondence to him carries the address Rabbi Abraham S. Yoe, Ph.D. or Dr. Abraham S. Yoe, with a salutation of Dear Dr. Yoe or Dear Rabbi Yoe being used.

No clergyman is ever addressed or introduced as Reverend or as Reverend Yoe. The term Reverend is an adjective, not a title. It should always be used in conjunction with a title, as exemplified in the previous paragraphs.

Private Usage

In the case of almost all clergymen and most nonclerical religious workers there is considerable, if not total, overlap between their professional and private activities.

Thus, the doctoral title, if used in professional life, will be carried over into private life.

Socially the clergyman will generally introduce himself with an ecclesiastical title or as Albert S. Yoe plus some information concerning his position. The social forms of address and introduction are the same as the professional ones detailed in the previous section.

Most clergymen have mail addressed to their homes with their titles, either ecclesiastical or doctoral, affixed. They are also thus known by salespeople, shopkeepers, and other commercial persons in their communities. Their titles may be carried on charge accounts, bank accounts, and credit cards if they desire, but many do not do so. Mailbox name plates may read The Rev. Albert S. Yoe or simply Albert S. Yoe.

On engraved and written formal invitations, acceptances, regrets, and announcements, proper ecclesiastical or doctoral titles should be employed. In informal notes, letters, and greetings, some use such titles and some do not, depending on the protocol in the various denominations. Social name cards may read The Reverend Dr. Albert Sarton Yoe or The Reverend Dr. and Mrs. Albert Sarton Yoe unless superseding ecclesiastical titles are used.

Other Professional Positions

Professional Usage

In addition to those mentioned, there are numerous persons holding doctor's degrees of various sorts who fall into two general professional categories. The first consists of those who are self-employed. Included in this category would be consulting chemists, geologists, physicists, biological scientists, engineers, and economists; clinical and testing psychologists; chemists, physicians, and engineers running special laboratories; private tutors in music and other fine arts; and some persons in business. The second of these categories includes doctorate holding employees of industrial and governmental organizations. These persons may be in research, control, analysis, or supervision.

For people in both categories, the doctorate stands as a sign that they have undergone a rigorous education for their positions. Since the degree thus is a mark of such a person's expertise, it is quite pertinent to his work. Therefore in all his professional relationships, he may write the degree initials after his name

RANDALL M. ROE, PH.D.

and may use the doctoral title before it.

DR. RANDALL M. ROE

At his work, he is addressed as Dr. Roe by personnel who come into contact with him. In the news media, when the report has to do with his professional activities, he is referred to as Dr. Randall M. Roe with material indicating directly or indirectly the type of doctorate he holds. When speaking before audiences on subjects relating to his specialty, he is introduced as Dr. Randall M. Roe, remarks being included describing his area of competence.

For those in private practice, the listing in the telephone directory is Roe Randall M with an indication of the profession added (psych, chem) and in some cases the degree initials. In the classified section, the degree initials may be added to the name. Outdoor signs, office door signs, and desk markers may follow the pattern of the name plus the degree designation plus a term or terms indicating the profession (Clinical Psychology, Engineering Consulting). Most scientists, psychologists, and engineers follow the above practices, but there is a tendency for persons holding doctorates in business, law, and the fine arts not to use the title. Nonetheless, a number do so, and this is a perfectly permissible practice.

For those in industrial and governmental employment, the telephone listing is simply Roe Randall M. Office door signs usually carry only the name, but desk markers may follow either of the patterns below.

RANDALL M. ROE, PH.D.
Research Associate

RANDALL M. ROE
Ph.D. (Biochemistry)

For those in private and in industrial and governmental employ, letterheads and business cards may carry the name with the degree initials added. The signature used by such persons may be *Randall M. Roe* written over the typewritten words Randall M. Roe, Ph.D., unless the latter appears elsewhere on the letterhead.

When letters are addressed to doctoral-holding persons in the above categories, both the envelope and inside addresses are written as Dr. Randall M. Roe or to Randall M. Roe, Ph.D., unless he is known not to use the title. The salutation reads Dear Dr. Roe.

Private Usage

The use of the doctoral title shows wide variation among persons who are self employed or employed by industrial or governmental organizations. Several professional organizations encourage their doctorate-holding members to use the title both professionally and socially. The general tendency appears to be for scientists, engineers, and psychologists to carry the title into their private lives, while others do not do so to so large a degree. Usually when friends discover a person to have a doctorate, they will so address him, unless he specifically objects. The use of the title depends on personal preference, the separation between professional and social activities, local custom, other persons involved, and the nature of the situation.

With regard to mail received at home, relations with tradespeople, banking activities, charge accounts, and other such things, a variety of practices exist. Mail box designations should read Randall M. Roe. On formal invitations, acceptances, regrets, and announcements, and on social cards, either Mr. or Dr. may be employed. Informal and personal communications sent to close friends carry simply the name.

It is important here to recall the remarks made earlier in the chapter. One should neither be ostentatious nor apologetic about the use of the title. One's personal preference and his feeling of comfort in the situations are probably the most important guides. The general tendency among persons mentioned in this section seems to have been an overly-apologetic one which has resulted from a fear of pretension. No such attitude is called for; the various earned doctorates represent a background of difficult work and accomplishment, giving a person every right to use the title if he chooses.

Foreign Countries

Examination of the usage of doctoral degree designations and titles in countries other than the United States reveals that in most of them all persons holding doctoral degrees are addressed both professionally and socially as Doctor. As has been indicated, many practitioners of medicine in a number of these countries do not hold doctoral degrees. In some countries, however, every person in medical practice is addressed as Doctor. The origin of this practice was indicated earlier in the present chapter.

Conclusion

Thus it may be seen that the basic rule provides a convenient guide to the usage of the doctoral degree and title.

If the expertise represented by a doctoral degree is pertinent to the situation, the title should be used, unless the holder of the degree prefers otherwise. If the expertise is not pertinent, the title may or may not be used, depending upon personal preference, local custom, and the degree of separation between the social and professional life of the possessor of the doctorate.

CHAPTER FOUR

The Ceremony of the Doctorate

Inasmuch as you have been presented to me for examination in Law by the Most Illustrious Daniel Dina, golden Knights, Counts Palatine, Most Celebrated Doctors, and inasmuch as you have since undergone an arduous and rigorous examination, in which you bore yourself with so much learning and distinction, thereby by the authority which I have, I name you Doctor of Law, giving you every privilege of lecturing, of ascending the master's chair, of writing glosses, of interpreting, of acting as advocate, and of exercising also the functions of a Doctor here and everywhere in the world.

— — — Adapted from an ancient University of Bologna commencement.

The Commencement

THE CEREMONY AT WHICH degrees are conferred by a college or university is known as commencement. This widespread custom is an exceptionally old one. It stems from the ancient ritual known as the inception, which was the ceremony recognizing a scholar as passing from studentship to that of teacher. It was therefore his commencement as a doctor or master in the university guild of teachers.

At Bologna, following a series of private qualifying examinations, the doctoral candidate was permitted to proceed to the public ceremony known as the inception. At this event he was given both the license to teach and the doctor's degree.

Prior to the appointed day the candidate extended

personal invitations to friends and public officials to attend the ceremony. On the appointed day, a procession made up of the candidate, his sponsoring doctor, some university officials, and the fellow students of his lodging house moved to the cathedral. Upon arrival, the aspiring doctor delivered a speech, then set forth a thesis in his area of study, and defended it against student questioners. He thereby played the part of the doctor for the first time.

Following his defense, the student was presented to a representative of the church and the faculty by his sponsor. The representative made a brief speech praising the candidate and then presented him with the license to teach. A formula something like that given at the beginning of this chapter was probably pronounced. The licensee was seated in the master's chair, was handed the open book (open to one of the texts it was his task to expound), a gold ring was placed on his finger, and the magisterial biretta was positioned on his head. The ceremony was concluded as the newly made doctor was paternally embraced, kissed, and given a benediction by his sponsor.

The procession then left the cathedral and paraded majestically through the town. The parade was often followed by a banquet to which all officials, colleagues, and university friends were invited. Finally, fees and gifts were extended to officials, doctors, marshals, and other dignitaries associated with the university. In many cases, the total cost was quite high, making it necessary for many students to delay their commencements for long periods of time.

The inceptions of other early universities resembled this ceremony in more or less detail. In some cases the order of the steps was altered, in others deletions and additions were involved. At some schools, the licensing and the being accepted as a member of the guild were separated into two ceremonies. These early inceptions underwent many changes as the years went by. Adaptations were made to apply the ceremony to a group of candidates rather than individuals. From these interesting beginnings has come the modern day graduation ceremony known as commencement.

Only in a few modern foreign universities does much of the old doctoral graduation ritual remain. In the majority it has almost completely disappeared. At the turn of the century Bologna and Padua used the ring, the Scottish universities employed the cap, the Swedish universities used a cap or a laurel and the ring, and Berlin employed the chair. As of about 1900, practically the full ancient ceremony could be seen in the Universities of Madrid, Coimbra, Louvain, and the Papal University in Rome.

Early Medieval Apparel

In modern day commencement exercises, doctoral candidates, as well as those being presented for other degrees, wear specially designed academic regalia. This costume usually consists of three articles: a gown, a hood, and a mortarboard cap. All three items have their histories rooted in the ordinary medieval apparel worn by almost all persons of the time.

In the twelfth century when the universities began to take shape, the dress of the people was quite different from that seen today. Practically everyone, both man and woman, wore as a basic article of apparel a long robe or gown. This gown varied in materials, cut, color, and trimmings according to the needs, position, and wealth of the wearer. In some areas, the designs of the gowns for persons of position and dignity were regulated by some sort of a code.

In addition to the gown, there were outer garments for

protection and warmth. Over the gown was worn a cloak which was often lined with fur, wool, or other heavy material and sometimes had a hood attached to it. The hood could be pulled up to cover the head or it could be left off to hang down the back. This outer garment, which has here been called a cloak, took many forms, closed and open, sleeved and sleeveless, girded and ungirded, pullover and slit with fastenings, and other variations.

From the thirteenth century, the hood was often absent from the cloak and was worn as a separate item. It was usually attached to a very short cape or shoulder piece which covered the shoulders and upper arms, the two together forming one garment. In many cases, a light undercap was worn, this usually taking the form of a simple, round, close-fitting headpiece. In general, then, the people of these times wore gowns, cloaks with hoods attached or cloaks plus separate hoods, and caps.

University Regalia

In the universities, the basic garments of early medieval wear (gown, cloak, hood, cap) were kept, with modifications. These changes produced a wide variety of costumes which underwent alteration from century to century.

Around 1450 in some schools, the small close-fitting cap became a fuller and looser circular bonnet. In other schools it took on a loose or rigid square style. The full, rigid biretta appeared in the following century, as did other styles of headdress, including the broad-brimmed hat. Tumps, apexes, stalks, tufts, and tassels were added to the different forms of caps in numerous places. In the sixteenth century in England, the headdress took the shape of a large, flat, shallow square cap, loose and drooping at the corners. A skull cap was worn under it, and in the next century the upper and lower caps were fastened to form one article. Not long afterward a board was inserted to keep the corners from falling.

In England the shoulder piece of the hood was gradually dispensed with. The utility of the hood was abandoned. It was lengthened, and silk linings came to replace the fur and the wool in many instances. On the Continent, both the hood and the shoulder piece often were given up and replaced by a shoulder scarf, which took many forms. This shoulder scarf had originated in a combination scarf-hat, the scarf having been attached to the shoulder so that the cap would hang down the sleeve or back when it was removed. In a few cases other devices were substituted for or worn in addition to hoods; these included bands, belts, sashes, collars, girdles, streamers, and tippets.

A tendency developed to wear the outer cloak open with the fur lining showing down the front or with the fur lining folded back down the front or used as a facing. In many instances, either the gown or the cloak was given up as a part of the regalia, leaving only three basic garments: the gown or cloak, the hood or scarf, and the cap. Velvet and fur came to be used for the collars and facings of some robes, and other adornments were added, such as buttons. braid, small symbols, and gimp.

In some countries, particularly in England, different types of academic dress for different occasions were prescribed. In certain schools, four different regalia were recognized for each doctorate, the festal dress, the congregation dress, the undress, and the chapel dress.

The Reformation and other radical societal changes often brought marked alterations in academic regalia. Very simple dress or the abandonment of all special university costume occurred at a number of schools, although subsequently elaboration or reinstatement gradually occurred.

Until around the middle of the fifteenth century, the cut or style of the academic regalia was the major factor which indicated the wearer's degree, both that it was a doctorate and the type of doctorate. Costumes of many colors had been worn but colors were not as important as style in most universities.

Gradually, however, in various schools certain colors came to be associated with the different fields of study, but an exact code was in force at only a few universities. A few decades later, by the early sixteenth century, general regulations were in effect in many places. The type of doctorate was indicated by color, different degrees taking different colors. The color appeared in the robes, or caps, or tassels or tufts on the caps, or hoods or scarfs, or two or more of these.

Each school had its own system. In 1440 at Aix, the caps were white (theology), violet (medicine), green (canon law), or red (civil law). As of 1547, at Valladolid the tassels on the caps were white (theology), yellow (medicine), blue (philosophy), green (canon law), and red (civil law). At Coimbra in 1580, distinctive colors the same as at Valladolid were used in the hood, tassels, and a ring. In Germany about this period, Erlangen and Leyden used orange (theology), green (medicine), white (philosophy), and red (law) for their robes.

Considering all the schools, white or black was favored for theology, yellow or violet or red for medicine, blue or violet for philosophy, and red for law.

Regalia in the United States

In the eighteenth century, academic costume was imported into this country from England by King's College and some other colonial institutions. These schools used the regalia in their graduation ceremonies and on other occasions. Gradually others adopted the practice, and by 1880 a fair number of institutions had codes in force. These included Columbia University, the University of Pennsylvania, Trinity College, St. John's College, University of the South, and Hobart College.

After 1880, a movement toward greater use of academic regalia began. By 1893, over thirty schools were employing some sort of ceremonial costume. In this year, an intercollegiate commission was formed to draft a uniform code for caps, gowns, and hoods. In 1895, it presented a set of standards, which was approved and led to widespread uniformity among schools in the United States. The code was amended slightly in 1932 and quite extensively in 1959.

Under the existing code, the gown for all doctor's degrees is made of black rayon, silk, or similar material. It is cut quite full, extends to within eight inches of the floor, and has wrist-length, bell-shaped sleeves. The gown has a full-length opening down the front center and is provided with fasteners so that it can be worn open or closed.

The garment is faced down both sides of the front center opening with bands of velvet about five inches wide which narrow and pass around back of the neck. On each sleeve, three horizontal velvet bars are placed. These are about two by fourteen inches and are spaced approximately two inches apart. The velvet of the facings and the bars may be black or of the color distinctive of the subject to which the degree pertains. These subject colors will be discussed later.

The doctoral hood communicates the maximum amount of information concerning the status of the wearer. It is made of black material identical in composition and weave with that used for the gown. The hood is looped over the head, hanging down in the back such that its lining will show. Its length of four feet differentiates it from the bachelor's and master's hoods which are shorter. The trimming of the hood is a five-inch band of velvet having the color distinctive of the subject to which the degree pertains. Hoods of bachelors and masters have narrower trimming. The lining of the hood carries the official color or colors of the awarding institution. More than one color is often shown by using one or two chevrons of the second color placed on top of the first color.

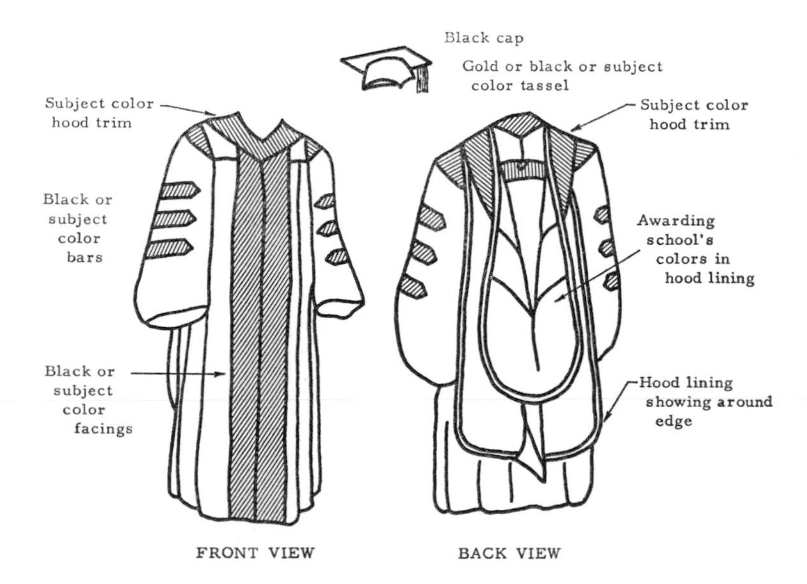

DOCTORAL ACADEMIC REGALIA

Another manner in which two colors can be shown is the parti per chevron arrangement. In this, one color is shown above the other, the border between them having the shape of a chevron. Other variations are employed including reversed chevrons, triple chevrons, the parti per chevron reversed, bars, and pales. One of the more interesting linings is that of The Carnegie Institute of Technology, which is tartan plaid. Hood linings of all major doctorate-granting institutions are listed in Appendix 2.

Thus the hood indicates the doctoral character of the degree (length of hood, width of trim), the general subject area in which the doctorate was given (color of trim), and the conferring institution (color of lining).

The cap is constructed of black material identical in composition and weave with that of the gown and the hood. Alternately, it may be of black velvet. It takes the familiar mortarboard form, although soft square-topped caps are permissible. A tassel is fastened to a button on the middle top of the cap. This tassel may be black, of gold thread, or of the color distinctive of the subject to which the degree pertains.

As has been noted, the trimmings of the gown may be black or of the subject color, the trimming of the hood is to be of the subject color, and the tassel on the cap may be black or of gold thread or of the subject color. Presented below is a chart of the subject colors now being used.

What is important in determining the proper subject color is the field of concentration of the study for the degree, not the degree itself. For example, all doctorates in agriculture (whether Ph.D., Ed.D., Sc.D., D.Agr., or other) have a subject color of maize. This would apply to a wide variety of fields of concentration such as agricultural education, vocational agriculture, animal husbandry, agronomy, dairy science, and horticulture.

All doctorates in engineering (whether Ph.D., Sc.D., Eng.D., or other) have a subject color of orange. Again a sizable number of fields would be included, examples being aeronautical engineering, ceramic engineering, chemical engineering, electrical engineering, and mechanical engineering. All doctorates in the sciences (whether Ph.D., Sc.D., or other) have a subject color of golden yellow. Included here would be the fields of biology, chemistry, geology, mathematics, and physics. Some would want to include psychology.

Subject Colors	
Agriculture	MAIZE
Arts, Letters, Humanities	WHITE
Commerce, Accountancy, Business	DRAB
Dentistry	LILAC
Economics	COPPER
Education	LIGHT BLUE
Engineering	ORANGE
Fine Arts, Architecture	BROWN
Forestry	RUSSET
Journalism	CRIMSON
Law	PURPLE
Library Science	LEMON
Medicine	GREEN
Music	PINK
Nursing	APRICOT
Optometry	SEAFOAM GREEN
Oratory, Speech	SILVER GRAY
Osteopathy	GREEN
Pharmacy	OLIVE GREEN
Philosophy	DARK BLUE
Physical Education	SAGE GREEN
Podiatry, Chiropody	NILE GREEN
Public Administration, Foreign Service	PEACOCK BLUE
Public Health	SALMON PINK
Science	GOLDEN YELLOW
Social Work	CITRON
Theology	SCARLET
Veterinary Science	GRAY

All doctorates in education have a subject color of light blue. Examples of fields involved here are art education, music education, science education, educational administration, secondary education, counseling and guidance, and philosophy of education. It should be noted that physical education has a color of its own.

The group of subjects known in most schools of the United States as the liberal arts or the arts presents an interesting ambiguity. These subjects (anthropology, archaeology, history, languages, literature, philosophy, political science, sociology, and sometimes mathematics and psychology) were what was historically included in the older universities under the faculty of arts or, as it was often known, the faculty of philosophy. Thus all these subjects could take the subject color of white (arts) or dark blue (philosophy). Since white is so readily soiled, dark blue is ordinarily chosen. The main exception seems to be in the case of honorary degrees (H.H.D., L.H.D., Litt.,D., Lit.D.) for which white is generally employed.

Similar principles can be applied to all university fields of knowledge to ascertain the proper subject colors. Listed below is a chart showing the most important fields in which doctorates are awarded. The subject has been ascertained in each case, and robe trim, hood trim, and tassel color options are given. The green for medicine, lilac for dentistry, and gray for veterinary science may be noted.

On the basis of these classifications, the faculty colors of a representative group of recent doctoral graduates run about 30 per cent green, 19 per cent golden yellow, 14 per cent lilac, 13 per cent dark blue, 7 per cent light blue, 5 per cent orange, 3 per cent gray, 2 per cent copper, 2 per cent maize, 1 per cent scarlet, 1 per cent silver gray, 1 per cent pink, and 2 per cent others.

GUIDE TO DOCTORAL GOWN TRIM, HOOD TRIM, AND TASSEL COLORS

Field	*Subject*	*Robe Trim*	*Hood Trim**
Agriculture	Agriculture	Black or maize	Maize
Anatomy	Science	Black or golden yellow	Golden yellow
Anthropology	Philosophy	Black or dark blue	Dark blue
Architecture	Fine Arts	Black or brown	Brown
Art	Fine Arts	Black or brown	Brown
Astronomy	Science	Black or golden yellow	Golden yellow
Bacteriology	Science	Black or golden yellow	Golden yellow
Biochemistry	Science	Black or golden yellow	Golden yellow
Biology	Science	Black or golden yellow	Golden yellow
Botany	Science	Black or golden yellow	Golden yellow

Field	*Subject*	*Robe Trim*	*Hood Trim**
Business Adm.	Commerce	Black or drab	Drab
Chemistry	Science	Black or golden yellow	Golden yellow
Dentistry	Dentistry	Black or lilac	Lilac
Divinity	Theology	Black or scarlet	Scarlet
Economics	Economics	Black or copper	Copper
Education	Education	Black or light blue	Light blue
Engineering	Engineering	Black or orange	Orange
Forestry	Forestry	Black or russet	Russet
Geography	Science	Black or golden yellow	Golden yellow
Geology	Science	Black or golden yellow	Golden yellow
History	Philosophy	Black or dark blue	Dark blue
Home Econ.	Economics	Black or copper	Copper
Journalism	Journalism	Black or crimson	Crimson
Languages	Philosophy	Black or dark blue	Dark blue
Law	Law	Black or purple	Purple
Letters	Arts	Black or white	White
Library Sci.	Lib. Sci.	Black or lemon	Lemon
Literature	Philosophy	Black or dark blue	Dark blue
Mathematics	Science	Black or golden yellow	Golden yellow
Medicine	Medicine	Black or green	Green
Music	Music	Black or pink	Pink
Nursing	Nursing	Black or apricot	Apricot
Optometry	Optometry	Black or seafoam green	Seafoam green
Osteopathy	Osteopathy	Black or green	Green
Pharmacy	Pharmacy	Black or olive green	Olive green
Philosophy	Philosophy	Black or dark blue	Dark blue
Physical Ed.	Phys. Ed.	Black or sage green	Sage green
Physics	Science	Black or golden yellow	Golden yellow
Physiology	Science	Black or golden yellow	Golden yellow
Podiatry	Podiatry	Black or nile green	Nile green
Pol. Sci.	Philosophy	Black or dark blue	Dark blue
Psychology	Philosophy	Black or dark blue	Dark blue
Public Adm.	Pub. Adm.	Black or peacock blue	Peacock blue
Public Hlth.	Pub. Adm.	Black or salmon pink	Salmon pink
Religion	Theology	Black or scarlet	Scarlet
Science	Science	Black or golden yellow	Golden yellow
Social Work	Soc. Work	Black or citron	Citron
Sociology	Philosophy	Black or dark blue	Dark blue
Speech	Oratory	Black or silver gray	Silver gray
Theatre	Oratory	Black or silver gray	Silver gray
Theology	Theology	Black or scarlet	Scarlet
Vet. Med.	Vet. Sci.	Black or gray	Gray
Zoology	Science	Black or golden yellow	Golden yellow

*Tassel may be black or gold thread or same color as hood trim.

For some fields of knowledge, a choice of colors is available. For example, one might notice religious education (scarlet or light blue), agricultural economics (maize or copper), nursing education (apricot or light blue), and engineering physics (orange or golden yellow). These allow choice because of their discipline-bridging character. Other fields allow choice because they are judged by some schools to be in one subject area and by others to be in another. Mathematics (golden yellow or dark blue) and psychology (golden yellow or dark blue) are examples of this situation.

For a number of years several institutions have employed a unique regalia of their own design. These may deviate slightly or widely from the code. Harvard University uses a crimson gown along with a specially designed black hood with crimson lining. A crow's foot in the subject color is worked into the lapels. Yale University utilizes a blue gown. Princeton University lines its black hood and decorates its black gown with orange, the second color of the school. Other schools wearing distinctive regalia include American University, Columbia University, Cornell University, Long Island University, New York University, Radcliffe College, and Tufts University.

The older code which was in force prior to 1959 called for the color of the hood trim and the optional color of the gown trim to correspond to the wording of the degree. That is, a Ph.D., regardless of the subject in which it was earned, indicated dark blue. The same table of colors was employed, but the appearance of one of the words in the table in the degree designation was determinative. The new code indicates that regalia manufactured under the old code may appropriately be used as long as they are in good condition, but that all new regalia should accord with the new specifications.

Conclusion

Thus there are hidden in the ceremony and the regalia of the doctorate much of its history, its present status, and its colorful character. The forms of the ceremony and regalia reflect the doctorate's origin and development. The many colors of the regalia trim illustrate its variety. The elaborateness of the regalia as compared to that of other degrees symbolizes its status as a mark of the highest academic attainment.

Appendixes

Appendix One

Abbreviations of Doctoral Degrees

A.Mus.D.	Doctor of Musical Arts[1]
D.Arch.	Doctor of Architecture[2]
D.B.A.	Doctor of Business Administration[2]
D.C.	Doctor of Chiropractic[1]
D.C.L.	Doctor of Civil Law[3]
D.C.S.	Doctor of Commercial Science[3]
D.Comp.L.	Doctor of Comparative Law[2]
D.D.	Doctor of Divinity[3]
D.D.S.	Doctor of Dental Surgery[1]
D.Ed.	Doctor of Education[2]
D.Eng.	Doctor of Engineering[2]
D.Eng.Sc.	Doctor of Engineering Science[2]
D.F.	Doctor of Forestry[1]
D.F.A.	Doctor of Fine Arts[3]
D.H.L.	Doctor of Hebrew Literature[1]
D.L.S.	Doctor of Library Science[1]
D.M.A.	Doctor of Musical Arts[1]
D.M.D.	Doctor of Dental Medicine[1]
D.M.L.	Doctor of Modern Languages[1]
D.M.S.	Doctor of Medieval Studies[1]
D.Mus.	Doctor of Music[2]
D.Mus.A.	Doctor of Musical Arts[1]
D.Mus.Ed.	Doctor of Musical Education[1]
D.O.	Doctor of Osteopathy[1]
D.P.A.	Doctor of Public Administration[2]
D.P.E.	Doctor of Physical Education[1]
D.P.H.	Doctor of Public Health[2]
D.Phys.Ed.	Doctor of Physical Education[1]
D.R.E.	Doctor of Religious Education[2]
D.S.C.	Doctor of Surgical Chiropody[2]
D.S.M.	Doctor of Sacred Music[2]
D.S.S.	Doctor of Social Science[illegible]
D.S.W.	Doctor of Social Work[1]
D.Sc.	Doctor of Science[2]
D.V.M.	Doctor of Veterinary Medicine[1]
Ed.D.	Doctor of Education[2]
Ed.R.D.	Doctor of Religious Education[2]
Eng.D.	Doctor of Engineering[2]
Eng.Sc.D.	Doctor of Science in Engineering[2]
J.C.D.	Doctor of Canon Law[2]

[1]Earned.
[2]Earned and honorary.
[3]Honorary.

J.D.	Doctor of Jurisprudence[2]	Mus.D.	Doctor of Music[2]
		O.D.	Doctor of Optometry[1]
J.S.D.	Doctor of the Science of Law[1]	Pd.D.	Doctor of Pedagogy[3]
		Ph.D.	Doctor of Philosophy[1]
L.H.D.	Doctor of Humane Letters[3]	Pharm.D.	Doctor of Pharmacy[2]
		Sc.D.	Doctor of Science[2]
Lit.D.	Doctor of Literature[3]	S.J.D.	Doctor of the Science of Law[2]
Litt.D.	Doctor of Letters[3]		
LL.D.	Doctor of Laws[3]	S.M.D.	Doctor of Sacred Music[2]
M.D.	Doctor of Medicine[1]	S.T.D.	Doctor of Sacred Theology[2]
Med.Sc.D.	Doctor of Medical Science[2]	Th.D.	Doctor of Theology[1]

Appendix Two

MAJOR DOCTORATE-GRANTING INSTITUTIONS AND THEIR HOOD COLORS

ADELPHI C. (N. Y.) : Ph.D. (Gold, brown chevron)
AKRON, U. OF (OHIO) : Ph.D. (Navy blue, old gold chevron)
ALABAMA, U. OF: Ph.D., M.D., D.D.S., D.Ed. (Crimson, white chevron)
ALASKA, U. OF: Ph.D. (Gold, royal blue chevron)
ALFRED U. (N. Y.) : Ph.D. (Purple, two old gold chevrons)
AMERICAN U. (D. C.) : Ph.D., Ed.D. (Red, white chevron, blue)
ARIZONA, U. OF: Ph.D., Ed.D., D.Mus.A. (National red, blue chevron)
ARIZONA STATE U.: Ed.D. (Maroon, gold chevron)
ARKANSAS, U. OF: Ph.D., M.D., Ed.D. (Cardinal, white chevron)
AUBURN U. (ALA.) : Ph.D., Ed.D., D.V.M. (Burnt orange, royal blue chevron)
BAYLOR U. (TEX.) : Ph.D., M.D., D.D.S., Ed.D. (Green, gold chevron)
BERKELEY BAPT. DIV. S. (CAL.) : Th.D. (Purple, gold chevron)
BOSTON C. (MASS.) : Ph.D., Ed.D. (Maroon, gold chevron)
BOSTON U. (MASS.) : Ph.D., M.D., Ed.D., A.Mus.D., Th.D. (Scarlet, white chevron)
BRANDEIS U. (MASS.) : Ph.D., D.S.W. (Wedgewood blue)
BRIGHAM YOUNG U. (UTAH) : Ph.D., Ed.D. (White above blue, parti per chevron)
BROOKLYN, POLYT. I. OF (N. Y.) : Ph.D., Eng.D. (Purple navy, gray chevron)
BROWN U. (R. I.) : Ph.D. (Seal brown, cardinal chevron)
BRYN MAWR C. (PA.) : Ph.D. (Old gold, white chevron)

BUFFALO, U. OF (N.Y.): Ph.D., M.D., D.D.S., Ed.D. (Yale blue, white chevron)

CALIFORNIA I. OF TECH.: Ph.D. (Orange, white chevron)

CALIFORNIA MEDICAL COLLEGE: M.D. (Gold, purple chevron)

CALIFORNIA PODIATRY C.: D.S.C. (Gold)

CALIFORNIA, U. OF: Ph.D., M.D., D.D.S., Ed.D., D.V.M., D.P.H., D.S.W., D.Eng., D.L.S., J.S.D. (Gold, yale blue chevron)

CARNEGIE I. OF TECH. (PA.): Ph.D. (Tartan)

CASE I. OF TECH. (OHIO): Ph.D., (Brown above white, parti per chevron)

CATHOLIC U. OF AM. (D. C.): Ph.D., Eng.D., D.Arch., S.T.D., J.C.D., D.S.W. (Yellow, white bar)

CHICAGO C. OF CHIROPODY (ILL.): D.S.C. (Purple, gold chevron)

CHICAGO C. OF OSTEOPATHY (ILL.): D.O. (Seafoam green)

CHICAGO LUTHERAN THEOL. SEMINARY (ILL.): Th.D. (Old gold above olive green, parti per chevron)

CHICAGO MEDICAL S. (ILL.): M.D. (Purple, gold chevron)

CHICAGO, U. OF (ILL.): Ph.D., M.D., J.S.D., D.Comp.L. (Maroon)

CINCINNATI, U. OF (OHIO): Ph.D., M.D., Ed.D., D.Sc., D.Ind. Med. (Bright red, two black chevrons)

CLAREMONT C. (CAL.): Ph.D. (Maroon, white chevron)

CLARK U. (MASS.): Ph.D. (White, emerald green chevron)

CLEMSON C. (S. C.): Ph.D. (Northwestern purple, burnt orange chevron)

COLORADO S. OF MINES: D.Sc.Eng. (Light navy above silver gray, parti per chevron)

COLORADO STATE C.: Ed.D. (Old gold, purple chevron)

COLORADO STATE U.: Ph.D., D.V.M. (Pumpkin yellow, alfalfa green chevron)

COLORADO, U. OF: Ph.D., M.D., Ed.D., D.B.A., D.Mus.A. (Gold, silver gray chevron)

COLUMBIA U. (N.Y.): Ph.D., M.D., D.D.S., Ed.D., D.P.H., D.S.W., Med.Sc.D., J.S.D., D.L.S., Eng.Sc.D. (Light blue, white chevron)

Connecticut, U. of: Ph.D. (National flag blue, white chevron)

Cornell U. (N. Y.): Ph.D., M.D., Ed.D., D.V.M., J.S.D., D.Sc. in Vet. Med., A.Mus.D. (Carnelian red, two white chevrons)

Creighton U. (Neb.): M.D., D.D.S. (light blue above white, parti per chevron)

Delaware, U. of: Ph.D. (Blue, golden yellow chevron)

Denver, U. of (Colo.): Ph.D., Ed.D. (Crimson, gold chevron)

Detroit, U. of (Mich.): D.D.S. (Cardinal above white, parti per chevron)

Drew, U. (N. J.): Ph.D. (Oxford blue, lincoln green chevron)

Dropsie C. (Pa.): Ph.D., Ed.D. (Yale blue, gold chevron)

Duke U. (N. C.): Ph.D., M.D., Ed.D., D.F. (Yale blue, white chevron)

Duquesne U. (Pa.): Ph.D. (Gules red, pale azure reversed chevron)

Emory U. (Ga.): Ph.D., M.D., D.D.S. (Blue, gold chevron)

Fairleigh Dickinson U. (N. J.): D.D.S. (Maroon, white chevron)

Florida State U.: Ph.D., Ed.D., D.Mus., D.Mus.Ed., D.Phys. Ed. (Garnet, gold chevron)

Florida, U. of: Ph.D., M.D., Ed.D. (Orange, blue chevron)

Fordham U. (N. Y.): Ph.D., Ed.D. (Maroon)

General Theol. Seminary (N.Y.): Th.D. (Scarlet hood, lined in purple)

George Peabody C. (Tenn.): Ph.D., Ed.D., D.Mus.Ed., D.P.E. (Garnet, turquoise chevron)

George Washington U. (D. C.): Ph.D., M.D., Ed.D., D.B.A., J.S.D., D.Sc. (Dark blue, buff chevron)

Georgetown U. (D. C.): Ph.D., M.D., D.D.S., S.J.D., D.Comp.L. (Confederate gray, union blue chevron)

Georgia I. of Tech.: Ph.D. (Old gold, white chevron)

Georgia, U. of: Ph.D., M.D., Ed.D., D.V.M. (Bright red above black, parti per chevron)

Hahnemann Med. C. (Pa.): Ph.D., M.D. (Blue, gold chevron)

HARTFORD SEMINARY FOUNDATION (CONN.): Ph.D., Ed.R.D. (Old gold)

HARVARD U. (MASS.): Ph.D., M.D., D.M.D., Ed.D., D.B.A., J.S.D., Med.Sc.D., D.P.A., D.P.H., D.Sc., Th.D. (Black hood lined in crimson)

HAWAII, U. OF: Ph.D. (Emerald green, two white chevrons)

HEBREW UNION C. (OHIO): Ph.D., D.H.L. (Old gold)

HOUSTON, U. OF (TEX.): Ph.D., Ed.D., O.D. (Red, white chevron)

HOWARD U. (D. C.): Ph.D., M.D., D.D.S. (Royal blue, white chevron)

IDAHO, U. OF: Ph.D., Ed.D., (Silver, two gold chevrons)

ILIFF S. OF THEOLOGY (COLO.): Th.D. (Light blue, white chevron)

ILLINOIS C. OF OPTOMETRY: O.D. (Royal blue, triple chevron of white, seafoam green, white)

ILLINOIS C. OF PODIATRY: D.S.C. (Purple, gold chevron)

ILLINOIS I. OF TECH.: Ph.D. (Scarlet, silver gray chevron)

ILLINOIS, U. OF: Ph.D., M.D., D.D.S., Ed.D., D.V.M., D.Mus. Ed., J.S.D., D.B.A., D.Mus.A. (Navy blue, two orange chevrons)

INDIANA U.: Ph.D., M.D., D.D.S., Ed.D., D.B.A., D.Mus.Ed., D.P.E., J.D., Dr. of Health Safety, Dr. of Recreation (Crimson, creme chevron)

IOWA STATE U.: Ph.D., D.V.M. (Old gold above cardinal, parti per chevron)

IOWA, U. OF: Ph.D., M.D., D.D.S., J.D. (Old gold)

JEFFERSON MED. C. (PA.): Ph.D., M.D. (Black, baby blue chevron)

JEWISH THEOL. SEMINARY (N. Y.): D.R.E., S.M.D., D.H.L. (Light blue, white chevron)

JOHNS HOPKINS U. (MD.): Ph.D., M.D., D.P.H., D.Eng., D.Sc. (Black, old gold chevron)

KANSAS CITY C. OF OSTEOPATHY AND SURGERY (MO.): D.O. (Purple, gold chevron)

KANSAS CITY, U. OF (MO.): Ph.D., D.D.S., D.Mus. (Royal blue, gold chevron)

KANSAS STATE U.: Ph.D., D.V.M. (Purple, two white chevrons)
KANSAS, U. OF: Ph.D., M.D., Ed.D. (Harvard crimson, yale blue chevron)
KENTUCKY, U. OF: Ph.D., Ed.D., Eng.D. (Blue, white chevron)
KIRKSVILLE C. OF OSTEOPATHY AND SURGERY (MO.): D.O. (Bright red)
LEHIGH U. (PA.): Ph.D., Ed.D. (Brown, two white chevrons)
LEWI C. OF PODIATRY (N. Y.): Pod.D. (Turquoise, gold chevron)
LOS ANGELES C. OF OPTOMETRY (CAL.): O.D. (Gold, purple chevron)
LOUISIANA STATE U.: Ph.D., M.D., Ed.D. (Purple, reversed gold chevron)
LOUISVILLE, U. OF (KY.): Ph.D., M.D., D.M.D. (Cardinal)
LOWELL TECH. I. (MASS.): Ph.D. (Red, black chevron)
LOYOLA U. (ILL.): Ph.D., M.D., D.D.S., Ed.D., S.T.D., J.D. (Maroon, gold chevron)
LOYOLA U. (LA.): D.D.S.
MAINE, U. OF: Ph.D. (Pale blue)
MARQUETTE U. (WIS.): Ph.D., M.D., D.D.S.
MARYLAND, U. OF: Ph.D., M.D., D.D.S., Ed.D., (Black, old gold chevron)
MASSACHUSETTS C. OF OPTOMETRY: O.D. (Maroon, silver gray chevron)
MASSACHUSETTS C. OF PHARM.: Ph.D. (Red, white chevron)
MASSACHUSETTS I. OF TECH. Ph.D., D.Sc. (Cardinal, reversed silver gray chevron)
MASSACHUSETTS, U. OF: Ph.D. (Maroon, white chevron)
MEDICAL EVANGELISTS, C. OF (CAL.): Ph.D., M.D., D.D.S. (Gold, purple chevron)
MEHARRY MED. C. (TENN.): M.D., D.D.S.
MIAMI, U. OF (FLA.): Ph.D., M.D., Ed.D. (Orange above, white chevron, green below)
MICHIGAN STATE U.: Ph.D., Ed.D., D.V.M., D.B.A. (Hunter green, white chevron)
MICHIGAN, U. OF: Ph.D., M.D., D.D.S., Ed.D., A.Mus.D., D.P.H., S.J.D., Pharm.D. (Maize, azure blue chevron)

MIDDLEBURY C. (VT.) : D.M.L. (Yale blue, white chevron)
MINNESOTA, U. OF: Ph.D., M.D., D.D.S., D.V.M. (Old gold, maroon chevron)
MISSISSIPPI SOUTHERN C.: Ph.D., Ed.D. (Spanish yellow, reversed black chevron)
MISSISSIPPI STATE U.: Ph.D. (White, maroon chevron)
MISSISSIPPI, U. OF: Ph.D., M.D., Ed.D. (Crimson, royal blue chevron)
MISSOURI, U. OF: Ph.D., M.D., Ed.D., D.V.M. (Old gold, two black chevrons)
MONTANA STATE C.: Ph.D., Ed.D. (Royal blue, reversed goldenrod chevron)
MONTANA STATE U.: Ph.D., D.Ed. (Copper, double bar, one silver, one gold)
NEBRASKA, U. OF: Ph.D., M.D., D.D.S., D.Ed. (Scarlet above cream, parti per chevron)
NEW HAMPSHIRE, U. OF: Ph.D. (Royal blue above white, parti per chevron)
NEW MEXICO HIGHLANDS U.: Ph.D. (Purple, white chevron)
NEW MEXICO I. OF MINING AND TECH.: Ph.D. (Silver, gold chevron)
NEW MEXICO STATE U.: Ph.D., D.Sc. (Crimson, white chevron)
NEW MEXICO, U. OF: Ph.D., Ed.D., D.Sc. (Silver gray, cherry red chevron)
NEW ORLEANS BAPT. THEOL. SEMINARY (LA.) : Th.D., D.R.E. (Purple, gold chevron)
NEW SCHOOL FOR SOCIAL RESEARCH (N.Y.) : Ph.D., D.S.S. (Emerald green, white chevron)
NEW YORK LAW SCHOOL: J.S.D. (Cherry red, black chevron)
NEW YORK MED. C.: M.D., D.P.H., Med.Sc.D. (Gold, reversed crimson chevron)
NEW YORK, STATE U. OF: Ph.D., M.D., Ed.D., Med.Sc.D. (Varies with the branch; blue, gold chevron most used)
NEW YORK U.: Ph.D., M.D., D.D.S., Ed.D., J.S.D., D.Eng. Sc., Med.Sc.D. (Violet)
NORTH CAROLINA C. AT DURHAM: Ph.D.
NORTH CAROLINA STATE C.: Ph.D. (Royal blue, gold chevron)

NORTH CAROLINA, U. OF: Ph.D., M.D., D.D.S., Ed.D., D.P.H. (Columbia blue, two white chevrons)

NORTH DAKOTA AG. C.: Ph.D. (Lemon yellow, grass green chevron)

NORTH DAKOTA, U. OF: Ph.D., Ed.D. (Pink, green chevron)

NORTH TEXAS, U. OF: Ph.D., Ed.D. (Kelly green, white chevron)

NORTHWESTERN U. (ILL.): Ph.D., M.D., D.D.S., D.Ed., D.Mus., D.J.S., J.D. (Purple, gold chevron)

NOTRE DAME, U. OF (IND.): Ph.D., D.Sc., D.S.M. (Old gold above royal blue, parti per chevron)

OCCIDENTAL C. (CAL.): Ph.D. (Orange, black chevron)

OHIO C. OF PODIATRY: D.S.C. (Kelly green collar, royal blue and gold streamers)

OHIO STATE U.: Ph.D., M.D., D.D.S., D.V.M., O.D. (Scarlet, silver gray chevron)

OHIO U.: Ph.D. (Green, reversed white chevron)

OKLAHOMA STATE U.: Ph.D., Ed.D., D.V.M. (Orange, black chevron)

OKLAHOMA, U. OF: Ph.D., M.D., Ed.D., D.B.A. (Crimson, cream chevron)

OREGON STATE U.: Ph.D., Ed.D. (Burnt orange)

OREGON, U. OF: Ph.D., M.D., D.D.S., D.Ed., D.B.A., J.D. (Lemon yellow, emerald green chevron)

OSTEOPATHIC MEDICINE AND SURGERY, C. OF (IOWA): D.O. (Purple, white chevron)

PACIFIC S. OF RELIGION (CAL.): Th.D. (Green, gold chevron)

PACIFIC, U. OF (CAL.): Ph.D., Ed.D. (Burnt orange, black chevron)

PACIFIC U. (ORE.): O.D. (Black, scarlet chevron)

PAPER CHEMISTRY, I. OF (WIS.): Ph.D. (White, two royal blue chevrons)

PENNSYLVANIA STATE C. OF OPTOMETRY: O.D. (Black, white chevron)

PENNSYLVANIA STATE U.: Ph.D., Ed.D. (Dark blue, white chevron)

PENNSYLVANIA, U. OF: Ph.D., M.D., D.D.S., Ed.D., V.M.D., D.S.W., J.S.D., Med.Sc.D. (Red, blue chevron)

PHILADELPHIA C. OF OSTEOPATHY (PA.): D.O. (Maroon, silver gray chevron)

PHILADELPHIA C. OF PHARM. (PA.): Ph.D. (Blue, white chevron)

PITTSBURGH, U. OF (PA.): Ph.D., M.D., D.D.S., Ed.D., D.P.H., D.S.W., D.Sc. (Navy blue, gold chevron)

PORTLAND, U. OF (ORE.): Ph.D., Ed.D. (Purple, white chevron)

PRINCETON U. (N. J.): Ph.D., Th.D. (Orange, black chevron)

PURDUE U. (IND.): Ph.D. (Black, two old gold chevrons)

RADCLIFFE C. (MASS.): Ph.D. (Crimson, white chevron)

REDLANDS, U. OF (CAL.): Ph.D. (Maroon, gray chevron)

RENSSELAER POLYTECH. I. (N. Y.): Ph.D., D.Eng.Sc. (Bright cherry red, white chevron)

RHODE ISLAND, U. OF: Ph.D. (White, Rhode Island blue chevron)

RICE U. (TEX.): Ph.D. (Blue, gray chevron)

ROCHESTER, U. OF (N. Y.): Ph.D., M.D., Ed.D., A.Mus.D. (Dandelion yellow)

ROCKEFELLER I. (N. Y.): Ph.D., Med.Sc.D. (Golden yellow, two royal blue chevrons)

RUTGERS U. (N. J.): Ph.D., Ed.D. (Scarlet)

ST. BONAVENTURE U. (N. Y.): Ph.D. (Brown, white chevron)

ST. JOHN'S U. (N. Y.): Ph.D., Ed.D., J.S.D.

ST. LOUIS U. (MO.): Ph.D., M.D., D.D.S. (White, yale blue chevron)

ST. MARY'S C. (IND.): Ph.D. (Light blue, white chevron)

ST. MARY'S SEMINARY AND U. (MD.): Th.D. (Pale blue, triple chevrons: gold, white, black)

SAN FRANCISCO THEOL. SEMINARY (CAL.): Th.D. (Scarlet above, yellow chevron, royal blue below)

SETON HALL U. (N. J.): M.D., D.D.S. (Yale blue, white chevron)

SMITH C. (MASS.): Ph.D. (White, gold chevron)

SOUTH CAROLINA, MED. C. OF: Ph.D., M.D. (Gold, black chevron)

SOUTH CAROLINA, U. OF: Ph.D. (Garnet, black chevron)

South Dakota State C.: Ph.D. (Light blue, two yellow chevrons)

South Dakota, State U. of: Ph.D., Ed.D. (Red)

Southern Baptist Theol. Seminary (Ky.): Th.D., S.T.D., D.R.E. (Gold, three reversed scarlet chevrons)

Southern California, U. of: Ph.D., M.D., D.D.S., Ed.D., D.B.A., D.M.A., D.P.A., D.S.W. (Gold, cardinal chevron)

Southern C. of Optometry (Tenn.): O.D. (Royal blue, gold chevron)

Southern Illinois U.: Ph.D. (Maroon, white chevron)

Southern Methodist U.: Ph.D., D.C.L. (Blue, red chevron)

Southwestern Bapt. Theol. Seminary (Tex.): Th.D., D.R.E. (Royal blue, white chevron)

Springfield C. (Mass.): D.P.E. (Maroon, white chevron)

Stanford U. (Cal.): Ph.D., M.D., Ed.D., J.S.D. (Cardinal)

Stevens I. of Tech. (N. J.): Ph.D., D.Sc. (Gray, red chevron)

Syracuse U. (N. Y.): Ph.D., EdD., D.B.A., D.P.A., D.S.S. (Orange)

Temple U. (Pa.): Ph.D., M.D., D.D.S., Ed.D., Med.Sc.D. (White, cherry red chevron)

Tennessee, U. of: Ph.D., M.D., D.D.S., Ed.D. (Orange, white chevron)

Texas, Ag. and Mech. C. of: Ph.D., D.V.M. (Maroon, white chevron)

Texas, U. of: Ph.D., M.D., D.D.S., D.Ed. (Orange, white chevron)

Texas Women's U.: Ph.D., Ed.D. (Maroon, white chevron)

Toledo, U. of (Ohio): Ph.D., Ed.D. (Dark blue, gold chevron)

Tufts, U. of (Mass.): Ph.D., M.D., D.M.D. (Brown, blue chevron)

Tulane U. (La.): Ph.D., M.D., D.P.H., J.S.D. (Olive green, light blue chevron)

Tuskegee I. (Ala.): D.V.M. (Crimson, gold chevron)

Union C. and U. (N. Y.): Ph.D., M.D. (Garnet)

Union Theol. Seminary (N. Y.): Ph.D., Th.D., S.M.D. (Scarlet)

UNION THEOL. SEMINARY (VA.) : Th.D. (Alice blue, white chevron)

UTAH STATE U.: Ph.D., Ed.D.

UTAH, U. OF: Ph.D., M.D., Ed.D. (Red, white chevron)

VANDERBILT U. (TENN.) : Ph.D., M.D. (Gold, black chevron)

VERMONT, U. OF: Ph.D., M.D. (Green, gold chevron)

VIRGINIA, MED. C. OF: Ph.D., M.D., D.D.S., Med.Sc.D. (Myrtle green, white chevron)

VIRGINIA POLYTECH. I.: Ph.D. (Orange, maroon chevron)

VIRGINIA, U. OF: Ph.D., M.D., Ed.D., J.S.D., D.Sc. (Navy blue, orange chevron)

WAKE FOREST C. (N. C.) : M.D.

WASHINGTON STATE U.: Ph.D., Ed.D., D.V.M. (Crimson above, silver gray below, parti per chevron)

WASHINGTON U. (MO.) : Ph.D., M.D., D.D.S., Ed.D., D.B.A., D.S.W., D.Sc. (Green, red chevron)

WASHINGTON, U. OF: Ph.D., M.D., D.D.S., Ed.D., D.B.A., (Purple above gold, parti per chevron)

WAYNE STATE U. (MICH.) : Ph.D., M.D., Ed.D. (Forest green, old gold chevron)

WEST VIRGINIA U.: Ph.D., Ed.D. (Old gold above navy blue, parti per chevron)

WESTERN RESERVE U. (OHIO) : Ph.D., M.D., D.D.S., D.Ed., D.S.W. (White, scarlet chevron)

WISCONSIN, U. OF: Ph.D., M.D. (Cardinal red)

WOMEN'S MED. C. (PA.) : M.D., Med.Sc.D. (Silver gray, scarlet chevron)

WOODSTOCK C. (MD.) : S.T.D. (Gold, white chevron)

WORCESTER POLYTECH. I. (MASS.) : Ph.D. (Gray, crimson chevron)

WYOMING, U. OF: Ph.D., Ed.D. (Brown, yellow chevron)

YALE U. (CONN.) : Ph.D., M.D., D.P.H., D.Eng., D.F., J.S.D, D.F.A. (Yale blue)

YESHIVA U. (N. Y.) : Ph.D., M.D., Ed.D., D.H.L. (Sky blue)

Appendix Three

Forms of Address for Higher Clergy of the Roman Catholic Church

CARDINAL	SPOKEN TO AS: Your Eminence. INTRODUCED AS: His Eminence, Albert Cardinal Yoe or Cardinal Yoe. WRITTEN ADDRESS AND PRINTED FORM: His Eminence, Albert Cardinal Yoe, S.T.D., Archbishop of Metro. SALUTATIONS: Your Eminence or Most Reverend Sir or Dear Cardinal Yoe.
ARCHBISHOP	SPOKEN TO AS: Your Excellency or Archbishop Yoe. INTRODUCED AS: His Excellency, Archbishop Yoe or Archbishop Yoe. WRITTEN ADDRESS AND PRINTED FORM: The Most Reverend Albert S. Yoe, S.T.D., Archbishop of Metro. SALUTATIONS: Your Excellency or Most Reverend Sir or Dear Archbishop Yoe.
BISHOP	SPOKEN TO AS: Your Excellency or Bishop Yoe. INTRODUCED AS: His Excellency, Bishop Yoe or Bishop Yoe. WRITTEN ADDRESS AND PRINTED FORM: The Most Reverend Albert S. Yoe, S.T.D., Bishop of Metro. SALUTATIONS: Your Excellency or Most Reverend Sir or Dear Bishop Yoe.
ABBOT	SPOKEN TO AND INTRODUCED AS: Father Abbot. WRITTEN ADDRESS AND PRINTED FORM: The Right Rev-

erend Albert S. Yoe, S.T.D., The Abbot of Metro. SALUTATIONS: Right Reverend Abbot or Dear Father Abbot.

MONSIGNOR SPOKEN TO AND INTRODUCED AS: Monsignor Yoe. WRITTEN ADDRESS AND PRINTED FORM: The Right (or Very*) Reverend Albert S. Yoe, S.T.D. SALUTATION: Dear Monsignor Yoe.

**Consult Official Catholic Directory for proper form.*

Appendix Four

FORMS OF ADDRESS FOR HIGHER
CLERGY OF THE PROTESTANT EPISCOPAL CHURCH

PRESIDING BISHOP	SPOKEN TO AND INTRODUCED AS: Bishop Yoe or Dr. Yoe. WRITTEN ADDRESS AND PRINTED FORM: The Most Reverend Albert S. Yoe, Th.D., Presiding Bishop of the Protestant Episcopal Church in America. SALUTATIONS: Most Reverend Sir or Dear Bishop Yoe.
BISHOP	SPOKEN TO AND INTRODUCED AS: Bishop Yoe or Dr. Yoe. WRITTEN ADDRESS AND PRINTED FORM: The Right Reverend Albert S. Yoe, Th.D., Bishop of Centralia. SALUTATIONS: Right Reverend Sir or Dear Bishop Yoe.
ARCHDEACON	SPOKEN TO AND INTRODUCED AS: Archdeacon Yoe or Dr. Yoe. WRITTEN ADDRESS AND PRINTED FORM: The Venerable Albert S. Yoe, Th.D., Archdeacon of Rural Work, Diocese of Centralia. SALUTATIONS: Venerable Sir or Dear Archdeacon Yoe.
DEAN	SPOKEN TO AND INTRODUCED AS: Dean Yoe or Dr. Yoe. WRITTEN ADDRESS AND PRINTED FORM: The Very Reverend Albert S. Yoe, Th.D., Dean of Centralia Cathedral. SALUTATIONS: Very Reverend Sir or Dear Dean Yoe.
CANON	SPOKEN TO AND INTRODUCED AS: Canon Yoe or Dr. Yoe. WRITTEN AD-

DRESS AND PRINTED FORM: The Rev. Albert S. Yoe, Th.D., Canon of Centralia Cathedral. SALUTATIONS: Reverend Sir or Dear Canon Yoe.

Appendix Five

Suggested
Business and Social Cards

JOHN R. COE, M.D.
Radiology

BY APPOINTMENT	1120 ALT BUILDING
TELEPHONE 579-8031	CLARE, OHIO 43407

ERIC G. NOE, D.V.M.
Veterinarian

8 A.M. TO 4 P.M.	8220 SOUTH DRIVE
TELEPHONE 703-9920	ARCO, IOWA 52348

DR. DALE B. POE
Professor of Botany

TELEPHONE 276-4228 EXTENSION 2021	METRO UNIVERSITY ARCO, IOWA 52348

THE REV. DR. ALBERT S. YOE
Pastor

TELEPHONE 722-8911	FIRST METHODIST CHURCH WALLINGTON, OREGON 97481

JAMES L. DOE, D.D.S.
Dentist

10 A.M. TO 4 P.M. TELEPHONE 367-4192	1012 ALT BUILDING CLARE, OHIO 43407

DALE B. POE, PH.D.
Professor of Botany

TELEPHONE 276-4228
EXTENSION 2021

METRO UNIVERSITY
ARCO, IOWA 52348

THE REV. ALBERT S. YOE, TH.D.
Minister

TELEPHONE
722-8911

CHRIST CHURCH
WALL, OREGON 97481

ABRAHAM S. YOE, D.H.L.
Rabbi

TELEPHONE
977-8102

TEMPLE BETH EL
HALLAN, NEW YORK 14862

THOMAS N. ZOE, PH.D.
Child Psychology

BY APPOINTMENT
TELEPHONE 481-9077

173 PLATT BUILDING
DOVE, MICHIGAN 48631

FLARY ELECTRONICS CORPORATION
Solid State Components

CARTER L. VOE, PH.D.
SOLID STATE RESEARCH

1712 MALLEY STREET
ORDEL, IDAHO 83852
TELEPHONE 297-4307

ROE ANALYTICAL LABORATORIES
Chemical Analysis

RANDALL M. ROE, PH.D.
ANALYTICAL CHEMIST

197 BENTON STREET
ARCO, IOWA 52348
TELEPHONE 931-7042

Doctor Eric Gregory Noe

Dr. and Mrs. Eric Gregory Noe

The Rev. Dr. Albert Sarton Yoe

Appendix Six

Manufacturers and Renters of Academic Regalia

Bentley and Simon, Inc.
7 West 36th Street
New York, New York 10018

Collegiate Cap and Gown Co.
1000 N. Market Street
Champaign, Illinois 61823

Cotrell and Leonard, Inc.
472 Broadway
Albany, New York 12201

E. R. Moore Co.
932 Dakin Street
Chicago, Ilinois 60613

The C. E. Ward Co.
New London, Ohio

Appendix Seven

A Brief Bibliography

Arminger, P.: *Titles and Forms of Address.* London, A. and C. Black, 1955.

Daly, L. J.: *The Medieval University.* New York, Sheed and Ward, 1961.

Eells, W. C.: *Degrees in Higher Education.* Washington, The Center for Applied Research in Education, 1963.

Eells, W. C., and Haswell, H. A.: *Academic Degrees.* Washington, U. S. Department of Health, Education, and Welfare, Office of Education, U. S. Government Printing Office, 1961.

Epler, S. W.: *Honorary Degrees, A Survey of Their Use and Abuse.* Washington, American Council on Public Affairs, 1943.

Foster, J. F., editor, *Commonwealth Universities Yearbook: 1960.* London, Association of Universities of the British Commonwealth, 1961.

Free, A. R.: *Social Usage.* New York, Appleton-Century-Crofts, 1960.

Hargreaves-Mawdsley, W. N.: *A History of Academical Dress in Europe Until the End of The Eighteenth Century.* New York, Oxford University Press, 1963.

Haycraft, F. W.: *Degrees and Hoods of the World's Universities and Colleges.* Cheshunt, Herts, Cheshunt Press, 1948.

Irwin, M., editor: *American Universities and Colleges.* Washington, American Council on Education, 1960.

Keyes, H. M. R., and Aitken, D. J., editors: *International Handbook of Universities.* Paris, International Association of Universities, 1962.

Malden, H.: *On the Origin of Universities and Academical Degrees*. London, Taylor, 1835.

Measures, H.: *Styles of Address*. Toronto, Macmillan of Canada, 1962.

Radlovic, I. M.: *Etiquette and Protocol*. New York, Harcourt, Brace, and Co., 1956.

Rashdall, H., Powicke, F. M., and Emden, A. B.: *The Universities of Europe in the Middle Ages*. New York, Oxford University Press, 1936.

Reid, R. H.: *American Degree Mills*. Washington, American Council on Education, 1959.

Schachner, N.: *The Medieval Universities*. New York, Frederick A. Stokes Company, 1938.

Sheard, K.: *Academic Heraldry in America*. Marquette, Northern Michigan College Press, 1962.

Thomas, F. S.: *University Degrees, What They Mean, What They Indicate, and How to Use Them*. New York, C. W. Bardeen, Syracuse, 1887.

Appendix Eight

Degree, Subject Color, and Academic Regalia Reform

At present over seventy different earned doctor's degrees and over seventy different honorary doctor's degrees are being awarded. Further, the designations of many doctorates do not adequately convey the general area of study. The situation at the bachelor's and master's levels is even worse. It is quite evident that degree reform is needed.

It is suggested that the following simplified system, if inaugurated would order things measurably and would in addition allow subject colors of academic regalia to match the degrees with exactness.

1) All holders of degrees in agriculture (agricultural chemistry, agricultural economics, agricultural education, agricultural engineering, agronomy, animal husbandry, animal science, dairy science, field crops, forestry, horticulture, poultry science, vocational agriculture, and other such subjects) will designate their degrees Ag.B., Ag.M., and Ag.D. (Subject color: maize)

2) All holders of degrees in the fine and applied arts (architecture, art, dramatic arts, music, speech) will designate their degrees A.B., A.M., A.D. (Subject color: pink)

3) All holders of degrees in the physical and biological sciences (anatomy, astronomy, bacteriology, biology, botany, chemistry, geography, microbiology, pharmacy,

physics, physiology, zoology, and other such areas) will designate their degrees Sc.B., Sc.M., Sc.D. (Subject color: golden yellow)

4) All holders of degrees in business subjects (accounting, advertising, business administration, commerce, commercial science, economics, finance, industrial management, marketing, secretarial science, transportation, and other such areas) will designate their degrees Bus.B., Bus.M., Bus.D. (Subject color: drab)

5) All holders of degrees in education (agricultural, art, business, childhood, commercial, elementary, health, home economics, higher, music, nursing physical, religious, science, secondary, speech, and vocational education, educational administration, guidance and counseling, and other such areas) will designate their degrees Ed.B., Ed.M., Ed.D. (Subject color: light blue)

6) All holders of degrees in engineering (aeronautical, agricultural, architectural, ceramic, chemical, civil, electrical, industrial, marine, mechanical, metallurgical, mining, petroleum, sanitary, and textile engineering and other such areas) will designate their degrees Eng.B., Eng.M., Eng.D. (Subject color: orange)

7) All holders of degrees in the liberal arts and behavioral sciences (anthropology, archaeology, English, French, German, Greek, history, journalism, languages, Latin, library science, linguistics, literature, mathematics, philosophy, political science, psychology, public administration, Russian, social work, sociology, Spanish) will designate their degrees Ph.B., Ph.M., Ph.D. (Subject color: dark blue)

8) All holders of degrees in law will designate their degrees LL.B., LL.M., LL.D. (Subject color: purple)

9) All holders of a doctorate in medicine will designate it M.D. (Subject color: green), in dentistry D.M.D.

(Subject color: lilac), in veterinary medicine V.M.D. (Subject color: gray)

10) All holders of degrees in theology and religion will designate their degrees Th.B., Th.M., Th.D. (Subject color: scarlet)

11) All holders of degrees in home economics (child development, clothing, family relations, foods, nutrition, textiles, and other such areas) will designate their degrees H.Ec.B., H.Ec.M., and H.Ec.D. (Subject color: white)

12) In abbreviations for all earned degrees, the degree initial will appear last. In abbreviations for all honorary degrees, the degree initial will appear first.

13) The following honorary degrees are recommended: in agriculture D.Ag., in fine and applied arts D.A. and D.Mus., in physical and biological sciences D.Sc., in business D.Bus., in education D.Ed., in engineering D.Eng., in liberal arts and behavioral sciences D.H.L. and D.Litt., in law D.LL., in the medical sciences D.Sc., in theology and religion D.D., in home economics D.H.Ec.

14) All present holders of degrees are to be asked to alter their degrees in accordance with the above canons and all colleges and universities are to agree upon awarding all future degrees according to these rules.

Reform toward simplicity is also called for in academic regalia. The most cumbersome and inconvenient part of academic costume is the hood. It is recommended that a very simple substitute be used instead of the present day bulky article. A light shield-shaped, V-shaped, or oblong-shaped piece of material (about 18 inches long and 12 inches wide) will be attached to the back of the gown about six inches below the shoulder line. It would be fixed only at the top, the sides and bottom remaining loose. Its color arrangements would resemble those now used for hood linings thus allowing the awarding school to be distinguished.

The gown would remain as it now is, except that the bars and facings on the gown would always be in the colors of the subject, no black option being appropriate.

The cap would also remain as it is now, except the tassel would always be in the subject color. The soft black square tam which is far more comfortable than the mortarboard would be an option.

SUGGESTIONS FOR HOOD REFORM

Index